AN

UNCOMMON

GUIDE

TO

Florida

Second Edition

A glove compartment companion for
residents, newcomers, and tourists.
Special things to do and see for all age groups.
Over 1,500 activities to help you explore the state's past,
present, and future. Take the uncommon tours and...
Florida will never look the same!

Nina McGuire

Second Edition

ISBN: 0–9631241–9–6

Welcome

Welcome to my Florida, a land of uncommon contrasts. The state's story is peopled with brilliant entrepreneurs, imaginative dreamers, and empire builders. These are the architects, town planners, artists, authors, composers, sports heroes, showmen, scoundrels, and "just plain folks" who created the Florida we see today. You'll meet them all in this book.

Each of the 24 uncommon tours can be accomplished in a few days. However, it is easily possible to spend weeks in each of the major areas described. Your time and budget considerations are the only limiting factors. The tours have been grouped for easy driving. All admission prices have been noted and are current as of 1997. Where pricing is not noted for young children, anticipate that they will be admitted at no charge. Be aware that many facilities are closed on some holidays. If you're unsure and if you're traveling during a holiday, it's always a good idea to phone ahead.

One of the aims of the book has been to help the traveler stay off tollroads and interstates. There is no negative implied in this statement. In urging you to travel the state's scenic byways, it is expected that you will discover many of your own personal, uncommon glimpses of our state. The back roads help you develop impressions of how the 20th-century has settled on land where prehistoric animals once roamed, where the country's oldest bald cypress tree took root 3,500 years ago, and where Indian nations made their homes. These routes take you to plantations, Civil War sites, pirate dens, space launches, attractions, and pristine beaches.

In this, the Second Edition of *An Uncommon Guide to Florida*, we have expanded the content to include even more of our favorite places. So, pull up a chair and decide what part of Florida you're ready to explore. We wish you good travels and hope that you...

Enjoy Florida.

Acknowledgments

M any friends and readers of the first edition of *An Uncommon Guide to Florida* have shared their Florida adventures with me. They have been generous with their time, energy, experience, and suggestions. Their comments and ideas have made this, the Second Edition, a better book. Thank you all.

W ithout the following state and federal organizations, this book could not have been written. Staff expertise, cooperation, research facilities, and encouragement made all the difference.

The Florida Department of Historic Preservation
The Florida Department of Natural Resources
The Florida Department of State
The Florida Department of Transportation
The Florida Department of Tourism
The Florida State Photographic Archives
The Florida State Archives
The U.S. National Park Service

S pecial thanks are due to friends who have provided invaluable assistance in the preparation of this edition. I am grateful to them all and would especially like to recognize the following. Sara Lee enthusiastically and tirelessly served as senior editor. Michele Caneen offered numerous thoughts and suggestions, particularly for the recreational selections. The ongoing and outstanding work and suggestions given by Melinda Horton at the Florida Association of Museums is appreciated. Of course, the efforts of the National Park Service, the State of Florida's Department of Natural Resources, and, particularly, the State of Florida's Department of Historic Preservation has been exceptional. The friendship and suggestions of Joan Morris and Joanna Norman at the Florida Photographic Archives made long hours of research feel like minutes. I thank them. Special thanks are due Mary Theuret of Typo–Graphics for her extra efforts. Mark Kellum and his team at Success by Design interpreted our ideas to make exactly the uncommon cover we had in mind. Thank you, also, to Barbara, Chris, Doug, Gene, Jan, John, Karen, Marilyn, Sam, Stuart, and Vicki who have provided invaluable assistance and support throughout stages of the development of this guide.

T hroughout the researching for this book, many Chamber of Commerce and Economic Development people throughout the state have offered suggestions and advice. Their help has been wonderful.

Although no one at any of the sites referenced knew a book was being written, I would like to thank the many people who staff our parks, museums, and other facilities. On a daily basis, they share their knowledge, excitement, and love of Florida. Their enthusiasm and skill in helping the rest of us understand the wealth of wonderful experiences in Florida's past, present, and future is contagious.

Writing this book has been an extraordinary experience. Although many have helped, the final book is my responsibility alone. No gratuities or other considerations have been received from any of the establishments mentioned. My criteria have been to select only those facilities which, to me, are outstanding, unique, and interesting enough to share with you.

My hope is that this small paperback book will find a place in your glove compartment as you tour Florida and create your own adventures and memories.

The book is dedicated to all those early residents and tourists who began development of the Florida we see today.

Tin Can Tourists at a Tampa Campground
Christmas Day, 1920

Table
of
Contents

Continued

The Uncommon Tours, continued

Gone Touring...
Panhandle Beaches

The Uncommon Tours

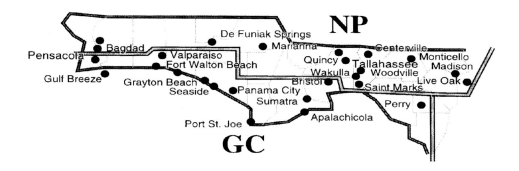

Florida is a wonderful state to explore! The book has been divided into eight major areas.

Northeastern Florida (NE)
East Central Florida (EC)
Southeastern Florida (SE)
Central Florida (C)
West Coast Florida (WC)
Gulf Coast Florida (GC)
Northern Panhandle (NP)
North Central Florida (NC)

Although each of the tours in the book is self–contained, the book has been designed so that most tours link with tours in connecting areas. The maps outlined in the book are provided as general reference points. Two maps which are particularly useful as armchair and auto companions are *Florida's Official Transportation Map* which is distributed through the State's Department of Commerce and the detailed *Florida Atlas & Gazetteer* which is available in many bookstores.

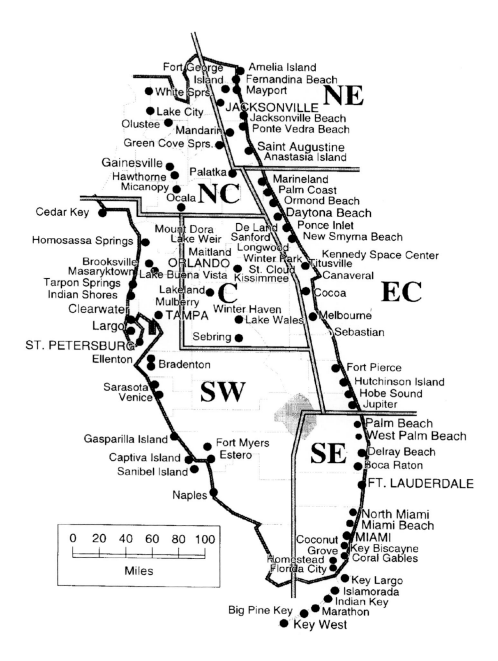

Fort George Island
Amelia Island
Fernandina Beach
White Sprs.
Mayport
Lake City
JACKSONVILLE
Jacksonville Beach
Olustee
Mandarin
Ponte Vedra Beach
Green Cove Sprs.
Saint Augustine
Anastasia Island
Gainesville
Palatka
Hawthorne
Marineland
Micanopy
Palm Coast
Ocala
NC
Ormond Beach
Cedar Key
Daytona Beach
Ponce Inlet
Mount Dora
De Land
New Smyrna Beach
Homosassa Springs
Lake Weir
Sanford
Maitland
Longwood
Kennedy Space Center
Brooksville
ORLANDO
Winter Park
Titusville
Masaryktown
Lake Buena Vista
St. Cloud
Canaveral
Tarpon Springs
Kissimmee
EC
Indian Shores
Lakeland
Cocoa
Clearwater
Mulberry
C
Largo
TAMPA
Winter Haven
Melbourne
ST. PETERSBURG
Lake Wales
Sebastian
Ellenton
Sebring
Bradenton
Fort Pierce
SW
Hutchinson Island
Sarasota
Hobe Sound
Venice
Jupiter
Palm Beach
Gasparilla Island
Fort Myers
West Palm Beach
Captiva Island
Estero
SE
Delray Beach
Sanibel Island
Boca Raton
FT. LAUDERDALE
Naples
North Miami
Miami Beach
Coconut
MIAMI
Grove
Key Biscayne
Homestead
Coral Gables
Florida City
Key Largo
Islamorada
Indian Key
Big Pine Key
Marathon
Key West
NE

0   20   40   60   80   100
Miles

9

Northeastern Florida

Northeastern Florida provides a beautiful study in contrasts. In a short distance the traveller moves from some of the quietest beaches in the state, to the oldest city in the nation, and then on to Jacksonville, the largest land mass city in the continental U.S. Two tour routes are highlighted for your enjoyment.

The Buccaneer's Trail begins on Amelia Island and travels south through Fernandina Beach, once one of the state's wealthiest communities. It crosses barrier islands and beautiful beaches before turning inland along the St. Johns River. While travelling west, there is a stop at the state's oldest plantation, a brief ferry ride to climb aboard a state–of–the–art naval vessel, a trip to the zoo, and a visit to the fascinating city of Jacksonville.

St. Augustine is *America's Oldest Settlement.* The historic city has been caringly restored. Skilled rangers and guides throughout the Old City introduce you to Florida's settlement as it was 400 years ago.

The return trip to Jacksonville ambles along the St. Johns River where steamboats travelled. Stop in Mandarin, the town where Harriett Beecher Stowe wrote of the post–Civil War period.

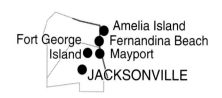

Tour 1.
The
Buccaneer's
Trail

Amelia Island – Fernandina Beach

As the state's northernmost island, Amelia Island became a safe haven for smugglers and pirates during the pre–Civil War days. The pirates would outrun Federal gunboats and land safely in the Florida Territory. During the Victorian period, the Island became the easternmost terminus for the state's first cross–state railroad. The combination of railroading and shipping made Amelia Island and Fernandina Beach desirable places to live. As you visit today, enjoy imagining life in the 19th century as you travel through the ***Centre Street Restoration*** area.

No one wanted to give up control of the Island. There were continuing feuds between buccaneers, settlers, and the U.S. Military. One way to understand these arguments is to explore ***Fort Clinch State Park.*** This unfinished pre–Civil War masonry and brick fort was started in 1847 as part of the coastal defense network to reduce the number of smugglers carrying goods to Confederate troops. The Fort was used during the Civil War and for training U.S. Troops during the Spanish–American War.

Bring your mountain bike to take advantage of the challenging bike trail. Travel through water pools and up steep hills to better appreciate the area! Also plan to visit during the first weekend of any month to experience a colorful, authentic reenactment of the Fort's 1864 occupation presented by rangers dressed as Union soldiers.

Location:	2601 Atlantic Avenue
Hours:	**Park**: Daily 8–sunset. **Fort**: Daily 9–5
Fees:	**Park:** $3.25 per car, maximum of 8 people per car
	Fort: $1
Phone:	(904) 277–7274

It's only a short drive along Route 105A from the Fort to Old Fernandina. Stop at the *Old Railroad Depot*, at First and Centre Streets, to get a walking tour booklet and explore the 30 block historic district.

The *Amelia Island Museum of History* offers a capsule view of the island's rich history from about 500 BC to 1910. Of particular interest is the 17th–century Spanish Mission display and the exhibit describing the Island's plantation life. There is also a section devoted to how railroading changed the island during the Victorian era.

Besides the on–site facility, the museum also sponsors walking tours through various parts of the community. Guides share interesting information about how history and the lives of residents intertwine. Bring your camera and wear comfortable walking shoes.

Location:	233 South Third Street
Hours:	**Museum Exhibition Hall:** Open Monday through Saturday at 11 and 2 for tours.
	Walking Tours: Centre Street Stroll on Thursday and Friday at 3 pm, starts daily from the Chamber of Commerce Courtyard, 102 Centre Street. **North and South Tours** are by 24–hour advance reservation only for groups of 4 or more. Each is two hours in length and begins at the Museum.
Fees:	**Museum:** Adults $2.50, students 6–21 $1.
	Walking Tours: Centre Street Stroll: Adults $5, students $4; **North Fernandina and South Fernandina Tours:** Adults $10 for each tour, students $5 for each tour
Phone:	(904) 261–7378

The water glows. The sun and clouds signal the end of day. The fleet floats home on a shimmering sea. Stop at the *Shrimp Docks,* at the foot of Centre Street, shortly before sunset and enjoy this sight. The drive along the Buccaneer's Trail continues. The route along Route 105 and A1A between Fernandina Beach and Fort George Island is one of the most scenic in the State. It is an area of natural beauty where magnificent quartz beaches, barrier islands, and tall dunes make it easy to enjoy solitude and majestic views. Travel slowly enough to allow time for lunch or a stay at the elegant *Amelia Island Plantation* or pause for a swim and picnic at *Little Talbot Island State Park.*

Fort George Island

If you had come from the Carolinas and Georgia in the first half of the 1800s and wanted to grow Sea Island cotton, it would be hard to find a better location than the *Kingsley Plantation Timucuan Preserve National Park.* The land was good, the climate was good, and the water access was exceptional. Zephaniah Kingsley bought the plantation for $7,000 in the early 1800s. He operated it for a quarter of a century.

The homestead, Florida's oldest plantation house, has been restored. To the rear of the main house is a two–story kitchen house, dating from 1792. South of the kitchen house is the stable and nearby are the remains of the crescent–shaped slave quarters, where over 100 slaves once lived. The self–guided interpretive displays of 19th–century plantation life are exceptional.

Location:	11676 Palmetto Avenue
Hours:	Daily 9–5
Fees:	No charge
Phone:	(904) 251–3537

The French landed at the site of what would become Fort Caroline in 1562, under the command of Jean Ribault. It marked the first attempt by the French to establish a presence in the western hemisphere. Their first attempt to settle the area failed, but the group returned two years later with 600 settlers. They successfully built the Fort Caroline settlement with the help of Timucuan Indians.

When the King of Spain heard about the French entering his territory, he sent Admiral Pedro Menéndez de Avilés and 500 soldiers to subdue them. They landed farther south along the coast. Jean Ribault and his troops heard of their arrival and sailed down the coast to attack them. There was a fierce storm. The Frenchmen were shipwrecked. Menéndez's troops captured Fort Caroline, killed the men who were there, and captured the women and children. On their way south, the Spaniards found the shipwrecked Ribault and 350 of his men. Every Frenchman was killed at the site now known as *Fort Matanzas National Monument*. The massacre ended France's attempt to colonize the area.

V isit *Fort Caroline National Memorial* to see the video and exhibits showing the French and Spanish struggle for control of territory in the "New World." Then take a walk along the trail in this beautifully wooded setting to see an interpretive model of the original fort.

Location:	12713 Fort Caroline Road
Hours:	Daily 9–5
Fees:	No charge, donations welcome
Phone:	(904) 641–7155

I t's just a short trip from Fort George Island along Highway 105 west to the *St. Johns River Ferry*. Take your car and enjoy a brief cruise on the St. Johns River!

Location:	Highway 105 west of Fort George Island, A1A at Mayport
Hours:	Daily 6:20 am to 10:15 pm
Fee (one way):	Car $2.50, person 50¢
Phone:	(904) 270–2520

Mayport

M ayport is one of the oldest fishing communities in the United States, dating back over 300 years. Although fishing is still important to the community, the Naval Station and the growth of the Jacksonville area have also had a major impact on the town.

A ll up and down the East Coast of Florida, lighthouses and houses of refuge were built to provide early warnings and safe havens for mariners in distress. Two interesting lighthouses can be seen at the *Mayport Naval Station.* The old *St. Johns Lighthouse* was built in 1859. Plans are now underway to open it as a museum. The new *St. Johns Lighthouse* dates from 1954. Although neither light is open for tours, make time to pause for a look at them. The seaward views are terrific and the glimpses of the Naval Station are interesting.

A weekend visit to the **Mayport Naval Station** is special! Depending upon which vessels are in port, you may be able to tour the **USS Boone**, the **USS Aubrey Fitch**, the **USS Farion,** or one of many other carriers for which Mayport is home port. Phone ahead for details concerning which carrier will be docked and available for touring when you're planning your visit. While you're there, be sure to ask if one of the guided–missile frigates is in port.

Location:	Check in at the Naval Station Security Building on Mayport Road
Hours:	**Carrier Tours**: Generally on Saturday 10–4, Sunday 1–4
Fees:	No charge
Phone:	(904) 270–5226

Although there are several ways to return to Jacksonville, it is suggested that you reboard the ferry and continue along the Buccaneer's Trail (Highway 105 west).

Jacksonville

Jacksonville began as a cow crossing in 1822 and is now a major metropolitan center. The community keeps growing. At last count, Jacksonville covered over 800 square miles and was the largest land area city in the lower 48 states. Known as a city of bridges, it is located within the double loop of the St. Johns River, the nation's longest north–flowing river. Throughout the book, we combine what you see-ing in "today's" Florida with images of "yester-day's" state.

*The sidewheeler, **City of Jacksonville**, departs from the Port of Jacksonville, bound down the St. Johns River, January 12, 1912*

People often went along the river for day trips. Wealthy Northerners traveled from Jacksonville by steamboat to enjoy winter holidays at the many springs near the St. Johns River. We can only imagine watching a steamboat round the bend. It is almost possible to hear a Stephen Foster melody slide across the water long after the boat had passed from sight.

*Sketch of the **Osceola** titled "General Grant in Florida- a trip on the Oklawaha," February 1880*

The *Jacksonville Zoological Gardens* houses more than 700 animals on over 60 acres. Begin your visit with a train tour to have an overview of the adventures ahead. Kids love the wonderful chimpanzee exhibit and the petting zoo. Give them plenty of time to plan their own adventures as you travel to the African Veldt. Who knows when they'll next meet a Great White Rhino?

Location:	8605 Zoo Parkway
Hours:	Daily 9–5, closed major holidays
Fees:	**Zoo:** Adults $6.50, seniors (over 65) $4.50, children 3–12 $4. **Train Tour:** Adults $3, children $2
Phone:	(904) 757–4463

Once downtown, take a moment to stop at one of the major hotels or the Chamber of Commerce for maps and detailed information about seasonal special events. Then enjoy a leisurely walk through the downtown area to admire the architecture, both old and new. Take an elevator ride to the top of one of the tallest buildings for a bird's–eye view of the bridges that link various parts of the Jacksonville area.

The formal portion of the Jacksonville tour continues with another child–oriented activity. The *Museum of Science and History* has three floors of scientific, historical, and anthropological exhibits. There are hands–on activities, a marine aquarium, and a state–of–the–art Alexander Brest Planetarium.

Two favorite activities at the museum are KIDSPACE, a play–with–me introduction to science designed for children up to 48" tall and Atlantic Tales and Marine Mammals, an interactive environment for learning about the habitats and hazards of sea creatures.

Location:	1025 Museum Circle
Hours:	Monday through Friday 10–5, Saturday 10–6, Sunday 1–6, closed major holidays
Fees:	Adults $6, seniors (over 65), active duty military personnel $4.50, and children 4–12 $3
Phone:	(904) 396–7062

Jacksonville prides itself on being a working class town so it is no surprise that there is a brewery here. But, what a brewery! The gigantic *Anheuser–Busch Brewery* covers 850 acres and produces over seven million barrels of beer a year. During the one hour tour visitors see the processes used to make beer (note that waste water from the manufacturing process is recycled and used at the Brewery's sod farm). You might want to plan this visit for an afternoon, choose a designated driver, and enjoy the tasting session after the tour.

Location:	111 Busch Drive
Hours:	Monday through Saturday 10–5, closed major holidays
Fees:	No charge
Phone:	(904) 751–0700

The *Cummer Museum of Art and Gardens* showcases the Wark Collection of early 18th–century Meissen porcelain, fine European and American art, and Japanese Netsuke. Be sure to see *Ponce de León in Florida*, an important and interesting painting recently purchased for $2 million. Another major reason to visit is the two acre, formal, waterfront garden modeled after an Italian period garden. The display in the garden changes seasonally and provides a refreshing pause before, during, or after a visit to the museum.

Location:	829 Riverside Avenue
Hours:	Tuesday and Thursday 10–9, Wednesday, Friday, and Saturday 10–5, Sunday 12–5, closed major holidays and 2 weeks in April
Fees:	Adults $5, seniors, students, and military $3. No charge on Tuesdays from 4–9
Phone:	(904) 356–6857

If you're interested in American history, the *Karples Manuscript Library* is a treasure chest. The collection is large and rotates among seven locations. When you step into the building you may see the proposal draft of the United States Bill of Rights, or the Emancipation Proclamation Amendment to the United States Constitution, or original drafts of the National Constitutions of France, Spain, and Mexico.

Location:	101 West First Street
Hours:	Monday through Saturday 10–3
Fees:	No charge
Phone:	(904) 356–2992

Each tour within the *Uncommon Guide to Florida* has been designed to connect to another fascinating part of the state. In the next section, you will walk along some of America's oldest streets.

St. Augustine streetscene, turn of the century.

Tour 2. America's Oldest Settlement

Tour 2 combines beaches, beautiful architecture, and history. The highlight of the tour is St. Augustine which is America's oldest, continuous settlement.

Ponte Vedra Beach

Although not well publicized, there are some fine public beaches along a 20 mile stretch of oceanfront between Ponte Vedra Beach and South Ponte Vedra Beach.

The area has had an interesting history. In 1916, two young chemical engineers sailed along the Coast looking for mineral–rich deposits. They came ashore at five to ten mile intervals between Brunswick, Georgia and Cape Canaveral, Florida to remove samples of beach sand. When their analysis was completed, the Ponte Vedra sand was judged to be best and a mineral processing plant was built.

During World War II, the Federal Government took over the plant and produced ilmenite and rutile, minerals that were used in the manufacture of munitions. Not surprisingly, the plant came to the attention of German military officers.

On June 16, 1942, a German submarine quietly surfaced off Ponte Vedra's shore. Four German soldiers were put into a rubber boat and rowed ashore. Beginning with the Ponte Vedra plant, their mission was to blow up several American defense plants. The Germans were seen, captured, tried, and found guilty. The plant continued production.

After the War, the plant and other properties were purchased by National Lead Company. Mining continued in the area until the State finally obtained an injunction and halted operations on the grounds that the beach, a public way, was being destroyed.

Ponte Vedra Lodge was built in 1927 to house plant employees. Step into the lobby and imagine that you're in a northwoods lodge. The original lodge now serves as the centerpiece of a beach, tennis, and golf resort. Although not inexpensive, this is a wonderful spot to spend a few days—or a few weeks. Bring a bike and a bathing suit and explore!

> Location: 200 Ponte Vedra Boulevard
> Phone: (904) 285–1111

St. Augustine

An important archaeological dig is underway just north of St. Augustine. It is slowly uncovering the location of *Fort Mosé*. In the late 1600s and early 1700s, slaves living on plantations in Georgia and North Carolina territories learned that slavery laws were less harsh in the Florida territory. Many African-born slaves braved swamps, storms, and alligators to travel south where Spanish colonists promised them sanctuary if they converted to Catholicism. By 1728, the Spanish governor of St. Augustine abolished slavery and freed African soldiers. Ten years later, in 1738, more than 100 African fugitives had arrived in St. Augustine from the English Carolina territory. The Spanish Governor of Florida established the fort and community of *Gracia Real de Santa Teresa de Mosé*. It bears the distinction of being America's first legally sanctioned free-Black community.

> Location: Off Highway A1A, two miles north of St. Augustine

St. Augustine is over 400 years old and is one of America's major historic and architectural treasures. Wear your most comfortable shoes and prepare to be a modern-day explorer. When you find a parking spot anywhere in the old city, take it! This is definitely a city that lends itself to leisurely walking. When you're tired of walking, you may want to continue the visit with a guided tram or horse–drawn carriage ride. In total, the area has 144 blocks on the National Register of Historic Places.

St. Augustine was founded in 1565. Spanish soldiers and their families struggled to survive in this isolated outpost. They built a wooden fort which offered limited protection for a little over a hundred years. However, in 1668 pirates swooped down, sacked the town, and killed 60 settlers. The surviving settlers decided to build a stronger fort, a *much* stronger fort. They constructed the **Castillo de San Marcos.** After it was built, they were never bothered by pirates again. The engineer was Ignacio Daza of Cuba.

The Castillo was built using new and unproven building techniques and an unknown local building material, coquina stone. Constructed between 1672 and 1695, the fort was built so well that it has never been conquered—although at various times it was occupied by Spanish, British, and U.S. Military forces. Many believe the fort's invulnerability is due to the unique, thick–walled architectural style and the use of coquina stone, quarried nearby. It is the nation's only remaining 17th-century masonry fort.

National Park Rangers talk of the fort's importance and tell tales of the struggles between the seven major adversaries who tried to control St. Augustine (Spain, France, England, American Indians—as well as American Revolutionaries, Confederates, and Northerners). As you walk through the fortress, realize that it has been in constant use for more than 300 years.

As European explorers and treasure ships sailed home-ward from the western hemisphere, the captains made use of the Gulf Stream current along St. Augustine's coast. The strategic location put the colony in the middle of continual power struggles. There were two wars as the English and Spanish forces fought over St. Augustine and its harbor. One siege lasted six weeks, the second lasted two months. During these periods, all of the area's settlers left their own homes and came to live in the open courtyard inside the fort. Imagine over 1,000 soldiers, townsmen, women, and children camping out in an area with no living quarters and only rudimentary cooking facilities.

When Havana fell to British forces in 1762, Spain, which had held Cuba, decided Cuba was more important than Florida. And so they traded Florida to Britain for the return of Cuba. The resident military group in St. Augustine changed. The Castillo was renamed the **Castle St. Mark**. British soldiers were based at the fort to maintain control of Florida during the Revolutionary War.

After the American Revolution, in 1783, Britain gave Florida back to Spain. As the U.S. grew, diplomats worked out a treaty with Spain and acquired Florida in 1821. More and more settlers moved to the territory and tension increased between the settlers and the Seminole Indians. Here and in other parts of the Florida territory this led to three devastating Indian Wars.

One of the most important leaders of the Seminoles was Osceola. He was not a chief, rather he was a spiritual leader. In October 1835, Osceola and 300 Seminoles were travelling under a white flag of truce. They were captured south of St. Augustine by U.S. Army troops who disregarded the white flag. The captives spent six weeks imprisoned at the fort. On November 29, 1835, 20 Indians slipped away and successfully escaped to the Everglades. The scandal from this escape prompted U.S. Army officers to take Osceola north to Ft. Moultrie in Charleston, South Carolina, where he died in January 1838. The Seminoles remaining in the fort were sent west to Indian territory in what is now Oklahoma.

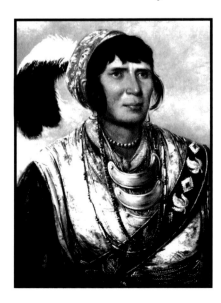

Shortly before President Abraham Lincoln was elected, Florida militia troops took over the fort. Cannons were hauled away to defend Jacksonville and the St. Johns River against Union gunboats. There was no fighting in St. Augustine during the Civil War, even though

Portrait of Osceola, painted from life by George Catlin. This was done at Ft. Moultrie, S.C. where Osceola was imprisoned.

both Confederate and Federal soldiers used the fortress. After the Civil War, Indians from the Great Plains and the southwest were held by the U.S. Army inside the fort. Captain Richard Pratt tried to give these captives an education instead of punishment. His efforts led to new Indian policies and the eventual establishment of the Carlisle Indian School in Carlisle, Pennsylvania. In 1924 the Castillo was declared a National Monument and the National Park Service was assigned its care in 1933.

Location:	One South Castillo Drive
Hours:	**Castillo**: Daily 8:45-4:45. **Ranger talks:** Daily usually at 10, 11, 2, and 3
Fees:	Adults $4, seniors over 62 with a Golden Age Passport and children under 16 no charge
Phone:	(904) 829–6506

Spanish colonial life is featured at the *Spanish Quarter Museum* which includes 10 restored or reconstructed colonial buildings from the 18th and 19th centuries. Be sure to see the Minorcan exhibit which includes a reconstruction of a kitchen dating from the Second Spanish period of around 1790.

Location:	Enter at the Triay House grape arbor, 29 St. George Street
Hours:	Daily 9–5, closed Christmas
Fees:	Adults $5, seniors over 62 $4.50, children 6–18 $2.50, or a family admission $10
Phone:	(904) 825–6830

Many Old City buildings are well worth seeing. The *Oldest House and Museum of Florida's Army* records life from the early 1700s, through British occupation, and to Henry Morrison Flagler's railroading era in the 1890s. It was continuously occupied from 1727 until 1918, when it was purchased by the St. Augustine Historical Society. It has been restored to reflect various periods throughout its long history.

Location:	14 St. Francis Street
Hours:	Daily 9–5, last tour of the day at 4:30, closed Christmas
Fees:	Adults $5, seniors over 55 $4.50, students $3, family of 2 adults and children under 18 $12
Phone:	(904) 824-2872

Henry Morrison Flagler

Henry Morrison Flagler was an important figure in Florida's 20th-century economic and agricultural expansion. While vacationing in St. Augustine, he decided to build a railroad and create hotels for wealthy Northerners. Before retiring to Florida, he had been senior lieutenant to John D. Rockefeller at Standard Oil Company. Whether he ever really retired is incidental. His impact on the state is major.

Imagine being surrounded by the contents of an early *Sears Catalog*. That feeling is reproduced at the *Oldest Store Museum* which was built in 1840. Many items date from the 1850s when the store supplied most of the building materials for Mr. Flagler's hotels. There are over 100,000 items, including a 1927 Model-T Ford. A good game for children is to ask them to find items they have never seen before, imagine how they would be used today, and then learn how they were used by our ancestors.

Location:	Four Artillery Lane
Hours:	Monday through Saturday 9–5, Sunday noon–5, closed Christmas
Fees:	Adults $4, children 6–12 $1.50
Phone:	(904) 829–9729

Another interesting stop, particularly with children, is the **Oldest Wooden Schoolhouse.** Built of red cedar and cypress between 1750 and 1773, it was put together with wooden pegs and handmade nails. The building became a school in 1804 and was used as a school for the next 60 years. Most kids enjoy seeing books used in schools before the Revolutionary War. They also learn that the schoolmaster and his family were never far away. In fact, they lived above the school.

Location:	14 St. George Street
Hours:	Daily 9–5, closed Christmas
Fees:	Adults $2, seniors and military with active military ID $1.50, children 6–12 $1
Phone:	(904) 824–0192

The *St. Photios Greek Orthodox National Shrine* preserves the history and memory of Greek colonists brought to Florida's east coast in 1768 who became part of the New Smyrna Colony. The building is known as the Avero House, built in 1749.

Location:	41 St. George Street
Hours:	Daily 9–5, closed Greek Orthodox Easter and Christmas
Fees:	No charge, donations welcome
Phone:	(904) 829-8205

Step inside the *Spanish Military Hospital* to see a ward, office, and apothecary dating from 1791. Step into the back yard to see a medicinal herb garden which is authentic for the period.

Location:	Aviles Street just off main square
Hours:	Daily 10-4, hours may vary
Fees:	No charge
Phone:	(904) 825–6830

Ponce de León had been the Spanish Governor of Puerto Rico. Always the explorer, he came to St. Augustine to find new land and to establish a new colony. He is said to have arrived on April 3, 1513. While exploring in Florida, he was supposed to have heard an old Indian legend about a spring whose water granted eternal youth. Although it is disappointing to accept, it must be emphasized that no literature suggests that he seriously looked for a fountain of youth—and, even worse, there is no evidence that he found one! Facts aside, step right up to the St. Augustine Aquifer at the the *Fountain of Youth* and you, too, can hope for a miracle.

On a more serious note, there is an excellent planetarium at the facility which shows ancient mysteries of navigation and the night skies as they would have appeared during the beginnings of the St. Augustine colony. There is also a brief film that tells of Spanish exploits along the coast, life–sized dioramas of Indian town life, and Ponce de León's landing.

Location:	11 Magnolia Avenue
Hours:	Daily 9–5, closed Christmas
Fees:	Adults $4.75, seniors over 60 $3.75, children 6–12 $1.75
Phone:	(904) 829–3168

America's first mission, *The Mission of Nombre de Dios*, was built in 1565. It commemorates the spot where Pedro Menéndez de Aviles, the founder of St. Augustine, celebrated North America's first mass. An important religious site, it reflects the beginning of the permanent history of Christianity in what is now the United States. A 208 foot tall cross marks the spot where the Spaniards planted the first cross.

Location:	27 Ocean Avenue
Hours:	Daily 9–6
Fees:	No charge, donations welcome
Phone:	(904) 824–2809

Otto C. Lightner, the founding editor of *Hobbies Magazine,* wintered in St. Augustine. In 1948, he converted the old *Alcazar Hotel* into the *Lightner Museum.* Today the museum contain his large collection of relics from America's Gilded Age. We particularly enjoy the Ballroom Gallery with its varied collection of paintings, furniture, and sculpture. However, if you only have time for a brief stop, go directly to the stained glass room designed by Louis Comfort Tiffany. In this area is an outstanding collection of American brilliant period and other Victorian stained glass.

Built in 1888, the hotel building is also impressive. When Henry Flagler built it, it was considered the less expensive place to stay as contrasted with the ***Ponce de León Hotel***, now Flagler College, directly across the street. The *Alcazar*, when built, had the largest enclosed swimming pool in the world. That area is now filled with an antique mall.

Location:	75 King Street at Cordova
Hours:	Daily 9–5, closed Christmas
Fees:	Adults $5, children $1
Phone:	(904) 824–2874

Henry Flager built the ***Memorial Presbyterian Church*** in 1890 as a memorial to his daughter who died giving birth to his granddaughter. The baby passed away 10 days later. Step inside this beautiful Venetian Renaissance Revival building for a quiet moment of reflection and to look at the stained glass windows he selected to grace their memories.

Location:	Valencia and Sevilla Streets
Hours:	Monday through Friday 8-5 or plan to attend services on Sunday morning at either 8:30 or 11
Fees:	No charge, donations welcome
Phone:	(904) 829–6451

Like the Oldest Schoolhouse, the ***Old Jail*** served two functions. Built by Henry Flagler in 1890, it was in continuous service as a jail until 1953. It housed criminals and included living quarters for the sheriff and his family. It is interesting to note that the sheriff's wife was expected to cook for the inmates. Besides viewing the building and learning how criminals were incarcerated in the late 1800s, make time to see the interesting collection of over 300 guns and other weaponry. Also at the same site is the ***Florida Heritage Museum*** which traces the area's history from the time of the Indians through the Flagler era.

Location:	167 San Marco Avenue
Hours:	Daily 8:30–5, closed major holidays
Fees:	**Each facility:** Adults $3.25, children 6–12 $2.25
Phone:	(904) 829–3800

Anastasia Island–St. Augustine Beach

Lighthouses were important along this section of the coast, particularly because of the treacherous currents and coral reefs. Constructed between 1871 and 1874, the *St. Augustine Lighthouse Museum* is housed in the restored Keeper's House and shows how lighthouse keepers and their families lived during that period. Climb the 219 steps and be rewarded with a panoramic view of sea, island, and St. Augustine.

Location:	81 Lighthouse Avenue
Hours:	**Museum:** Daily 9:30–5, **Lighthouse:** Daily 10-4:30, closed major holidays
Fees:	Adults $4, seniors $3, military no charge, children over 7 $2
Phone:	(904) 829–0745

When the Spanish settled St. Augustine, they crossed the Matanzas River to Anastasia Island where they quarried a local building rock called coquina. The quarry is part of the *Anastasia State Recreation Area* which covers over 1,700 acres of ancient oaks and sand dunes. During the 16th– and 17th–centuries, coquina was one of the most important building materials used in northeastern Florida. Not particularly attractive, its pitted, oyster shell appearance belies extraordinary strength.

Location:	300 Anastasia Park Drive
Hours:	Daily, 8–sunset
Fees:	$3.25 per car, maximum of 8 people per car
Phone:	(904) 461–2033

If you're in the area between mid–June and late August, be sure to see Florida's State Play, *Cross and Sword*. This performance is staged in an outdoor amphitheater and has a cast of over 50 actors, musicians, and dancers. During the two hour performance, the audience travels to Spain, the world of King Philip II, and the founding of what is now the United States. Join Captain Pedro Menéndez de Aviles and his Spanish crew as they set foot on these shores on September 8, 1565 and learn about the world they discovered, and the world they created.

Location:	1340 A1A South
Hours:	Monday through Saturday evenings at 8:30 from **mid–June through late August**
Fees:	Adults $8, seniors (over 65) $7, students (if over 16, ID is required) $4
Phone:	(904) 471–1965

Remember French Admiral Jean Ribault, founder of Fort Caroline on Fort George Island? A visit to the *Fort Matanzas National Monument* is the site where Admiral Ribault and 350 of his soldiers were slaughtered by Spanish Admiral Pedro Menéndez de Aviles in 1564. The word "matanzas" means "slaughter." The battle marked the first European contest for control of the New World.

Two hundred years later, the English, under the command of General James Oglethorpe, blocked the entrance to the Matanzas River at St. Augustine. His hope was that the Spanish would run out of supplies and surrender. General Oglethorpe gave up when he realized that Spanish supply ships from Havana had entered the river here, the "Southern back door" waterway to St. Augustine. However, this experience caused the Spanish to replace a small existing wooden watch tower at this site with the stone fort, built in 1742, at this site.

This is a beautiful place to visit. Walk the nature trail and take the ferry ride across the Matanzas River. Be sure to stop at the Visitor's Center and see the video.

Location:	8635 A1A South
Hours:	**Fort**: Daily 8:30-5. **Ferry**: Daily 9-4:30
Fees:	No charge
Phone:	(904) 471-0116

Mandarin

Harriet Beecher Stowe and her family wintered in Mandarin for many years, beginning in the 1880s. Although best known as the author of *Uncle Tom's Cabin,* she wrote *Palmetto Leaves* in her Mandarin home at 12447 Mandarin Road. The book describes the Reconstruction Period after the Civil War.

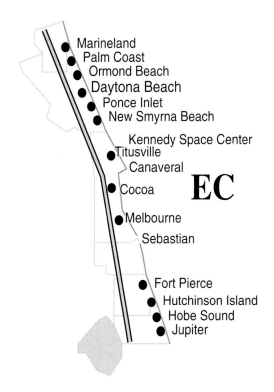

Marineland
Palm Coast
Ormond Beach
Daytona Beach
Ponce Inlet
New Smyrna Beach
Kennedy Space Center
Titusville
Canaveral
Cocoa **EC**
Melbourne
Sebastian
Fort Pierce
Hutchinson Island
Hobe Sound
Jupiter

East Central Florida

Travelling along A1A down the East Coast of Florida continues the study in contrasts discussed in the earlier tours.

Millionaires, Sand, and Auto Speed Records provides a look backward. Millionaires were among the first people to own automobiles. They spent their holidays refining cars and then breaking all speed records. This was first done on the sands at Ormond Beach. Tour 3 recognizes one of Florida's particularly illustrious winter citizens. We pause to remember just plain "Neighbor John," known to millions as John D. Rockefeller.

Most first–time visitors to East Central Florida head to *The Space Coast,* described in Tour 4. The *Astronauts Memorial*, rockets, movies, and a bus trip to the launching pad provide days of interesting touring.

Many longtime winter residents travel to Hutchinson Island, Hobe Sound, and Jupiter Inlet. The history of these areas began along *Lighthouse Row.* Since the 16th–century, many ships have been lost off these shores. If you're adventuresome, go to the library to learn about the ship wrecks, and then go scuba diving. Even if you don't find a treasure, being in the water and exploring a 17th–century wreck certainly counts as a treasure of a day!

Marineland
Palm Coast
Ormond Beach

Tour 3.
Millionaires, Sand,
and
Auto Speed Records

Marineland

The original marine life attraction in Florida is *Marineland of Florida*. When tanks were stocked in May 1938, experts had no experience understanding which species could live together. After some trial and error, the surviving fish began to thrive in the first oceanarium. Today's features include dolphin shows, a 3–D movie, and the oceanarium. We particularly enjoy the Secrets of the Reef and Wonders of the Springs exhibits. The Cayman Pit is filled with interesting and unusual South American alligators. Although there are many locations in contemporary Florida to watch marine life, this facility is an important example of how the technology began.

Location:	9507 Oceanshore Boulevard (A1A)
Hours:	Daily 9–5:30, shows begin at 9:15
Fees:	Adults $14.95, seniors over 65 $11.95, students 13–18 $9.95, children 3–12 $7.95
Phone:	(800) 824–4218 (FL), (800) 874–0492 (U.S.) (904) 471–1111

Palm Coast

Over 390 acres along the Atlantic Ocean and the Matanzas River have been preserved at the *Washington Oaks State Gardens*. Begin your visit on the ocean side. Along the picturesque, boulder strewn beach, the waves have washed away sand exposing a stratum of coquina rock. Try to plan your visit at low tide to watch many species of shorebirds find dinner around the rocks. This is a good spot for a picnic to enjoy the peace of the riverfront setting, the variety of everchanging gardens, and the vibrancy of the beach setting.

Location:	6400 North Oceanshore Boulevard (A1A)
Hours:	Daily 8–sunset. **Tours**: Saturday and Sunday at 1:30
Fees:	$3.25 for car, maximum of 8 people per car
Phone:	(904) 446-6780

Ormond Beach

In 1875, the Corbin Lock Company of New Britain, Connecticut established Ormond as a health center for employees threatened with tuberculosis. By the latter part of the 19th–century, the area became a millionaire's playground. The toys for this beachfront sandbox included the newest toy of all, the emerging gasoline powered automobiles. International millionaires brought their cars, their cars' designers, and their stop watches. Speed tests were held regularly on the firmly packed sand. Ormond claims to be the birthplace of speed. In 1906, a Stanley Steamer driven by Fred Marriott was clocked at 127.66 miles per hour. In 1935, the *Bluebird* reached 276 miles per hour, with Sir Malcolm Campbell driving.

John D. Rockefeller founded Standard Oil Co. and Henry Morrison Flagler was one of his senior lieutenants. They each retired to Florida. For years, John D. Rockefeller had said Ormond Beach was the healthiest place on earth. It is not surprising that Henry Flagler decided to build a hotel in the city, the Hotel Ormond. Opposite the hotel's golf course, the city's most famous citizen, John D. Rockefeller, purchased *Casements*, a small and

unpretentious house. In other parts of the world, John D. Rockefeller was known as a ruthless, vigorous, relentless businessman. Particularly as he grew older, the greatest of the trust builders was recognized by townspeople simply as quiet Neighbor John.

John D. Rockefeller at a fair in Ormond Beach, 1926

He spent his winters at *Casements* from 1914 until his death in 1937. Known as the Rockefeller House, it had been built in the early 1900s in a shingled-style. Most of the casement windows overlook the Halifax River. Although it is somewhat austere today, think of its three story entrance decorated with a Tiffany stained glass skylight, velvet draperies, and formal gardens to recall the Rockefeller era. The home has been restored and now contains both a small museum and a community center. In addition to information about Mr. Rockefeller, this unusual museum has one of the largest Boy Scout exhibits in the country. There is also a beautiful collection of Hungarian folk art reflecting the area's large Hungarian population.

Location:	25 Riverside Drive
Hours:	**Museum:** Monday through Thursday 9–9, Friday 9–5, Saturday 9–noon, closed holidays. **Tours:** Monday through Friday 10-2:30, Saturday 10-11:30
Fees:	No charge, donations welcome
Phone:	(904) 676–3216

Opposite Casements is *River Bridge*, once the *Ormond Union Church.* Following services, Mr. Rockefeller often stood on the lawn and distributed bright, shiny, new dimes to eager neighborhood children. With the dimes, the children received a mini sermon outlining the importance of thrift and savings if they wanted to build a fortune.

If you're ready for a brief pause, plan to visit the *Ormond Memorial Art Museum and Gardens.* The four and a half acre botanical garden was designed after World War II by returning servicemen. Make time to slowly wander the nature trails and find the fish ponds. The museum has a small and interesting collection, highlighted by the symbolic religious paintings of Malcolm Fraser.

Location:	78 East Granada Boulevard
Hours:	Monday through Friday 10–4, Saturday and Sunday 12–4
Fees:	No charge, $2 donation requested
Phone:	(904) 676–3347

"...start your engines!"
Twenty-two local racers at the starting line,
Daytona Beach races, January 14, 1905
grow to become
serious sport at the Daytona Speedway, 1977

Tour 4.
The Space Frontier

Speed and distance records are destined to be broken. Beginning in the early 20th–century, auto and motorcycle records have been made and shattered time and time again. As America's space program developed, this area grew to be one of the major sites from which rockets and shuttles were launched. Tours, exhibits, movies, museums, and an exquisite and moving *Astronaut Memorial* help us appreciate the impact and importance of space exploration.

Daytona Beach

Daytona has been known for setting auto racing records since the turn of the century. During the first decade of the 20th–century, the world's speed record of 68 miles per hour, established in 1903 by Andrew Winton, was broken a number of times. In 1910, a new measured mile world record was set on the Daytona Beach sands at 131.72 miles per hour by Barney Oldfield. The early races, held on hardpacked sand along the beach, attracted a world–class group of serious speedsters and their automobiles.

Today, the beach has been reclaimed by swimmers, surfers, sunbathers, and their cars. This is one of the few places in Florida where, for a small fee, you can take your family, your picnic, your umbrella, your volleyball, your frisbee, and your vehicle to spend a day at the beach. Enjoy yourself and remember to watch your car at high tide!

Barney Oldfield in the Blitzen Benz, Daytona Beach, 1910.

The Blitzen Benz was built in France specifically to challenge the Stanley Steamer. On March 16, 1910, Barney Oldfield flew through the measured mile time traps to set a new world record of 131.72 miles per hour.

The hot spot in Florida for racing and learning about racing is the ***Daytona International Speedway***. Plan your first visit on a day when no race is scheduled. Start at ***DAYTONA USA, The Ultimate Motor Sports Attraction.*** We suggest beginning your visit with a tram tour to learn about the Speedway, go into the pits, and onto the rim road at the very top of the track. An amazing experience. Once off the tram, enjoy looking at the famous racing cars. To get an idea of how grueling the Daytona 500 can be, the winning car is on exhibit—just as it looked as it finished the last lap. If you think you are pretty good with cars, step up for the Sixteen Second Pit Stop Challenge and try being part of a pit crew, The Technology of Speed machine takes apart super–racer Jeff Gordon's car so you can see why it's so fast.

Now that you've been behind the scenes, plan another visit and spend an exciting day watching intense competitors and amazing machines. Call ahead to make race reservations. And to think this race with speed all started on Ormond Beach and Daytona Beach.

Location:	1801 West International Speedway Boulevard
Hours:	Daily 9–7, closed Chirstmas.
Fees:	**DAYTONA USA:** Adults $12, seniors over 60 and children over 12 $10, children 6–12 $6. **Tram Tours:** $6
Phone:	**DAYTONA USA:** (904) 947–6800. **Speedway Tickets:** (904) 253–RACE

Another place to see wonderful memorabilia from the early days of auto racing is the *Halifax Historical Society and Museum*, located in a 1911 bank building. Begin your visit with the video showing the development of the area. We especially enjoy the miniature replica of the Daytona Beach boardwalk showing how the beach area looked in the late 1930s.

Location:	252 South Beach Street
Hours:	Tuesday through Saturday 10–4, closed major holidays
Fees:	Adults $2, children under 12 50¢
Phone:	(904) 255–6976

As you begin a trip down the Space Coast, stop at *Embry–Riddle University*. It is fitting that a school devoted solely to the study of aviation should be located along the Space Coast. Phone ahead for reservations for an interesting campus tour. Depending upon class schedules, you may be able to see the flight line operations, a wind tunnel, and flight simulators.

Location:	600 South Clyde Morris Boulevard
Hours:	**General Campus Tours:** Daily 10, 12, 2.
	Aeronautical Science Tour: Daily 10, 12, 2
Fees:	No charge
Phone:	(904) 226–6000

Throughout Tour 4, the conquering of new frontiers will be described. Of the pioneers described in this book, Dr. Mary McLeod Bethune is one of the most important. Daughter of a freed slave, she had a vision to create an academy for African–American women students. She knew what the school could be and was single–minded in sharing that vision with others. Although she had no money, she helped a generation of supporters, benefactors, students, and statesmen understand her idea, help her expand it, and benefit from her dream. The one room academy opened in 1904 and has grown into the *Bethune–Cookman College* campus

Dr. Mary McLeod Bethune, ca. 1915

you see today. The tour provides an interesting counterpoint between the fine work of an American educational pioneer and the fine education at today's college. We especially appreciate that the tour includes Dr. Bethune's home showing how she lived, her books, and papers.

Location: 640 Second Avenue
Hours: Monday through Friday 9–5 when school is open
Fees: No charge
Phone: (904) 255–1401

Located in the 60 acre Tuscawilla Park Reserve, the *Museum of Arts and Sciences* has recently opened a new wing dedicated to international decorative arts from 16th– to 20th–centuries. We particularly call your attention to the Louis Comfort Tiffany collection. In the science section, children always enjoy looking at the skeleton of a giant ground sloth, estimated to be 130,000 years old. Its remains were found near the museum grounds and show us one of Florida's earliest visitors.

General Fulgencio Batista was president of Cuba from 1940–1944 and 1952–1958 and vacationed at Daytona Beach. His family donated their paintings and artifacts to the museum. The Cuban Gallery houses the largest collection of Cuban art in the U.S. There are fine examples of 18th–century Spanish Colonial art, 19th–century impressionism, folk art, and 20th–century modern art.

Location:	1040 Museum Boulevard
Hours:	**Museum**: Tuesday through Friday 9–4, Saturday and Sunday 12–5, closed major holidays.
	Planetarium shows: Tuesday through Friday at 2, Saturday and Sunday at 1 and 3
Fees:	**Museum**: Adults $4, students and children $1, Saturday, no charge. **Planetarium:** $2
Phone:	(904) 255–0285

Ponce Inlet

The 175 foot tall *Ponce de León Inlet Lighthouse* was built in 1884. It was dark for a time. After being relit in 1982, its beam can now be seen for 95 miles between St. Augustine and Cape Canaveral. Climb the 203 steps to the topmost area open to visitors and enjoy a spectacular panoramic view of the inlet, the land, and the sea. The 15 minute video tells the history of the area.

Ponce de León Inlet Lighthouse

There are seven buildings to explore, including the lighthouse keeper's cottages which display navigational instruments, turn–of–the century furnishings, and the light's original lens.

Location:	4931 South Peninsula Drive
Hours:	**September through April:** Daily 10–4. **May through August:** Daily 10–9
Fees:	Adults $4, children 2–11 $1
Phone:	(904) 761–1821

New Smyrna Beach

An early Indian village named Caparaca was once located in this area. It is believed that Ponce de León landed near the village in 1513. The first large, well–recorded European settlement in the area occurred about 250 years later when a group of over 1,000 Scottish, Greek, and Italian settlers arrived in 1767. They stayed for nine years and moved on after years of dealing with hurricanes, Indian attacks, and what was to them an unfamiliar and inhospitable natural environment.

You may want to pick up a copy of *The Open Boat*, by Stephen Crane. This makes particularly good beachside reading in this area since Mr. Crane was shipwrecked just off the coast in 1897. He was rescued in a small lifeboat which drifted toward Daytona Beach. The wooden boat broke apart near shore. Fortunately, he was rescued again. His gripping narrative gives one increased respect for the weather, the shoals, and the hazards of ocean travel in those days. It also serves as a quiet reminder of the role played by the lighthouse keepers and the men we will meet in the next tour who staffed the Houses of Refuge along the shore.

Mr. Crane's experience notwithstanding, New Smyrna Beach is one of the safest spots to swim along this coast. There is a protective rock ledge well offshore that reduces the force of the undercurrents reaching the beach. So, if you're in the mood for an ocean swim, and are traveling with younger children, pause here.

Merritt Island

The tour now moves from outer space to surface space as we explore the next frontier. The mission of the **Merritt Island National Wildlife Refuge** is to preserve endangered species. The site and staff do it very well as this 140,000 acre refuge is home to more endangered species than any other area of the continental U.S. Begin your visit with a drive along the seven mile Black Point Wildlife Drive for a self–guided look at the major habitats within the refuge. Many people suggest that the best time for a first visit is between November and March when the migratory birds are in the refuge, with January and February being the peak season for wood storks, roseate spoonbills, scrub jays, and red shouldered hawks. Look up to see Southern bald eagles overhead.

Location:	Highway 402, 4 miles east of Titusville
Hours:	Daily 8–4:30
Fees:	No charge
Phone:	(407) 861–0667

John F. Kennedy Space Center

Before we even talk about the extraordinary things to do and see at the **Kennedy Space Center**, let's discuss logistics. First, immediately after you arrive, purchase tickets for the bus tour and an IMAX show. Consider visiting the **Astronaut Memorial** early in the day to pay homage to U.S. Astronauts who gave their lives to further space exploration.

The narrated bus tour includes the giant Vehicle Assembly Building, which houses space shuttles, and the towering launch pad where Neil Armstrong took his last great steps on Earth before his giant leap on the moon in 1969. There are massive six million pound crawler transporters that carry space shuttles to their launch pads. Tour the Flight Crew Training Building with its Apollo 11 Moon Landing Show. There is a stop at the *Air Force Space and Missile Museum* and the opportunity to see the sites where the first astronauts were launched in the Mercury and Gemini programs.

The *Apollo–Saturn V Center* is NASA's only museum designed to showcase the achievements of Project Apollo. The center houses spaceflight equipment. The 363 foot Saturn V moon rocket was the most powerful rocket ever built, producing more than 7.5 million pounds of thrust upon blast–off, and is only one of three moon rockets in existence. The cutaway model of the rocket is impressive. Apollo artifacts on display include the command module used in the July 1975 Apollo–Soyuz mission and Jim Lovell's space suit from the Apollo 13 mission. Exhibits and films reveal the emotion of the pioneering days of the Apollo era such as

the building and testing of the massive rocket, rigorous astronaut training, and the ultimate success of landing on the moon and returning safely to Earth.

Presentations in the Firing Room Theater and Lunar Surface Theater are exceptional. In addition, the New Frontiers Gallery features hands–on exhibits, including computer–generated

...and launch!

simulations of planetary explorations, tours of the solar system, and drives across the surface of Mars.

The museums have rich collections. Try to make time to see the *Gallery of Spaceflight Museum*. It includes such items as a Gemini space suit, a full–size model of a Lunar Rover, and a moon rock. The NASA Art Gallery shows more than 250 paintings and sculptures created by artists commissioned by the NASA Art Program. The Rocket Garden is an impressive way to realize the advances made in rocketry. Satellites and You is a 45 minute exhibit that uses robotic astronauts to demonstrate how satellites affect life on earth...and there are wonderful IMAX films. We suggest several visits to even begin to understand the magnitude of the important work being done at the Kennedy Space Center.

Location:	Kennedy Space Center, Route 405
Hours:	Daily 9:45–two hours before sunset, closed Christmas and during certain periods on launch days
Fees:	**Bus Tours**: Adults $8, children 3–11 $5. **IMAX Film**: Adults $4, children 3–11 $1.75
Phone:	(407) 452–2121

Titusville

The Mercury astronauts are featured within the *United States Astronaut Hall of Fame*. Videotapes of Mercury flight segments are shown. They help bring the era to life as do the personal mementos, notes from space, and equipment donated by the astronauts. It's special fun to use the simulators to try to land a shuttle and the centrifuge that replicates a jet fighter's flight. Astronaut Adventure is an interactive exhibit, You will experience a 3–D aerial combat mission, land a space shuttle, pull up to 4Gs in the centrifuge, and float in a virtual reality version of Skylab. Just another exciting day on the Space Coast!

Location:	6225 Vectorspace Boulevard
Hours:	Daily 9–5, closed Christmas
Fees:	Adults $9.95, seniors $8.95, children 5–12 $5.95
Phone:	(407) 269–6101

At some point during their childhood, many youngsters dream of life on other planets and traveling in space. The *U.S.*

Space Camp provides a chance for fourth through seventh graders to *almost* experience space. The five day summer program teaches the history of the American space program through hands–on activities—including a simulated space shuttle mission.

Some adults never stop wishing they could travel into space. Bring your youngster and become part of the Parent–Child Weekend Camp. When you check in you receive a space log, live "on board," eat astronaut food, build a launch rocket, experience a space simulation—and do it all in a weekend. If interested, book your space adventure well in advance.

Location:	6225 Vectorspace Boulevard
Hours and Fees:	**Space camp**: Fees per participant $675
	Parent/Child Weekend: Per parent/child team $600
Phone:	(407) 269–6100

At the ***Valiant Air Command Warbird Air Museum*** it is possible to see a U.S. Navy space simulator and restored planes. The museum contains a wide range of artifacts from World War I through the Vietnam era. It also shows military aircraft history of all nations. The exhibits help visitors understand the major contribution the military has made to civilian aviation development and the safety of modern flights.

Location:	6600 Tico Road, Space Center Executive Airport
Hours:	Daily 10–6, closed major holidays
Fees:	Adults $6, seniors over 60 and military with ID $5, children under 13 $4
Phone:	(407) 268–1941

Canaveral

One of the last truly undeveloped beaches on the East Coast is part of the ***Canaveral National Seashore***. The area is a sanctuary for at least 15 endangered species as well as winter quarters for thousands of migratory birds. The setting is natural. Should you go? Absolutely—but only when you have time to stop wearing a watch and start watching the environment. As you enter the Seashore, stop at the Ranger Station for detailed information.

Earlier cultures lived in this area and there are still at least 60 undeveloped sites dating from the Indian and Spanish settlement periods. Head north to look for Turtle Mound, an Indian oyster shell midden. This mound was the highest point of land for miles around and served as an important landmark on 16th–century maps. If you canoe, try the two mile canoe trail through Mosquito Lagoon. Bring your mosquito repellant. Playalinda Beach is particularly beautiful with its shifting sands and sea oats.

Location:	US 1 North to Garden Street, East to the Beach
Hours:	**Late April through late October**: Daily 6 am–8 pm. **November through mid–April**: 6–6, **Playalinda Beach**: closed three days preceding a launch and the day of a launch
Fees:	$3.25 per vehicle with up to 8 passengers. Walk–in visitors and bikers $1. Golden Age Passport for citizens 62 and older, lifetime pass $10
Phone:	(407) 267–1110

Cocoa

Who would name a town after a breakfast drink? There's an interesting and supposedly true story to be told. Originally called Indian River City, the U.S. Post Office told the townspeople their community's name was too long. They had to change it. What a problem! Everyone had a favorite name. Finally, a meeting was held in the general store. Names were presented and rejected all evening. No consensus was reached. As the meeting was about to break up, someone noticed a tin of cocoa on the store's shelf. As a joke, the suggestion was made that the town be named Cocoa. They liked it, and voted it in, and—we presume—went home for a commemorative cup of cocoa.

The *Astronaut Memorial Space Planetarium and Observatory* has the state's largest public access telescope. It is a 24 inch telescope. There is a model of John Glenn's space capsule in the Science Quest hall and the Planetarium is home to the only Minolta Infinium Star Projector in the Western Hemisphere.

Location:	1519 Clearlake Road, Brevard Community College
Hours:	**Museum and Planetarium:** Tuesday, Friday, Saturday 6:30–9pm. **Observatory:** Same hours as above (weather permitting). **Laser Show:** Friday and Saturday 9 and 10:30 pm
Fees:	**Exhibits and Observatory**: No charge. **Plan–**

etarium: Single Show: Adults $4, seniors over 59 and students $3, children under 12 $2. **Both shows:** Adults $7, seniors over 59 and students $5, children under 12 $4. **Laser Show:** $7

Phone:	(407) 634–3732

Melbourne

Liberty Bell Memorial Museum houses the uncracked replica of the Liberty Bell, cast by London's Whitechapel Bell Foundry in 1976, weighing 2,080 pounds. There are replicas of the twelve flags of the Revolutionary War period as well as 32 full–scale reproductions of historic documents, including the draft of the Declaration of Independence, the Mayflower Compact, and the Japanese Surrender Document following World War II.

Location:	1601 Oak Street
Hours:	Monday through Friday 10–4, Saturday 10–2
Fees:	No charge
Phone:	(407) 727–1776

Melbourne Beach

The eleven mile strip of coast between Melbourne Beach and Sebastian Inlet is the nation's largest nesting area for endangered loggerhead sea turtles. From late May through September, it is possible to spend an evening watching sea turtles lumber ashore to deposit eggs in the sand. Sea turtle watches are planned by the Audubon Society and nature and science centers along this part of the coastline as well as on Merritt Island, Hutchinson Island, Jensen Beach, and Sebastian Inlet.

Sebastian Inlet

In July of 1715, eleven fully loaded treasure ships, part of the Spanish Plate Fleet, left Cuba for Spain. Blown off course by a terrible hurricane, all the boats were wrecked off the Sebastian shore. A survivor's camp was set up on the site of what is now the ***McLarty State Museum***. Runners went up and down the beach to find the sailors. In this way, 1,500 people were saved. From 1715 through 1719, the survivors, aided by Ais Indians living in the area,

45

worked at salvage operations to regain part of the sunken treasure. Many golden and silver items found were shipped back to Spain. However, many treasures were not recovered. Within the museum there are dioramas showing how the survivors lived, as well as artifacts of the Ais Indians and the 1715 shipwreck. Plan to see the excellent 25 minute movie telling the story of modern-day salvaging. Then go out to the observation deck, shaped like a ship, and see where salvaging takes place.

Location:	13180 North A1A
Hours:	Daily 10–4:30
Fees:	General admission $1
Phone:	(407) 589–2147

Pelican Island is the nation's oldest wildlife sanctuary and was established in 1903 by President Theodore Roosevelt. No visitors are permitted, so please anchor near the shore to observe the birds and animals. If you have questions, phone the Merritt Island National Wildlife Refuge at (407) 861–0667.

Pelicans enjoying another sunny day in Florida

Fort Pierce
Hutchinson Island
Hobe Sound
Tequesta
Jupiter

Tour 5.
Lighthouse
Row

As you may have noticed, the character of the Atlantic coastline changes from tour to tour and the area covered along Lighthouse Row tour is no exception. For people who enjoy quiet elegance and beautiful natural scenery, this stretch of beach may become an all–time favorite.

Fort Pierce

A fascinating stop is the ***Harbor Branch Oceanographic Institution***. This natural history facility preserves plants and sea life from the ocean and estuaries. Make time to see the research vessel and the small aquariums. Oh, and of course, pause to see the lifelike sculpture by Seward Johnson whose family began the facility.

Location:	5600 US 1 North
Hours:	Monday through Friday 9-6, Saturday 9-5, Sunday 12-4, closed holidays
Fees:	Adults $5, children $3
Phone:	(561) 465-2400

During World War II, underwater demolition teams of the U.S. Navy trained in the area. Their contribution to the war effort is highlighted at the ***Underwater Demolition Team–SEAL Museum***. Be sure to see the video presentation highlighting training processes used and the exhibits tracing the exploits of Navy divers from 1944 to astronaut landings at sea. Displays include former top secret midget submarines and an Iranian gun boat that was captured in the Persian Gulf in the 1980s.

Location:	3300 North State Road A1A
Hours:	Tuesday through Saturday 10–4, Sunday 12–4
Fees:	Adults $3.25, children 6–12, $1.50
Phone:	(561) 595-5845

Hutchinson Island

Several American inventors came to Florida at the turn of the century. One who lived and worked in the area was Sterling Elliott. He is perhaps best known for inventing the first addressing machine. The *Eliott Museum Historical Memorial* features his inventions as well as reproductions of fourteen early American shops and inventions covering the period from 1865–1930.

Location:	825 Northeast Ocean Boulevard
Hours:	Daily 11-4, closed major holidays
Fees:	Adults $4, children 6–13 50¢
Phone:	(561) 225–1961

One of the most important locations along this coast at the turn of the century was the *Gilbert's Bar House of Refuge*. The two-story shingled house was built in 1875. Ironically, it was named for Don Pedro Gilbert, a notorious pirate who operated on the waterways in the area during the early 19th-century. In the late 1800s, ship captains had to rely on maps and visual sightings to avoid the treacherous hidden reefs along the Atlantic Coast. They were also at the mercy of fierce storms common during some seasons of the year. This is the only house of refuge remaining of the ten that were originally built along the east coast. It was deactivated in 1945.

The Gilbert's Bar House of Refuge opened under the care of keeper Fred Whitehead. He patrolled the beach each morning and after storms. When he found shipwrecked sailors, he took them back to the House of Refuge and cared for them until they were well. A dormitory on the second floor housed the rescued sailors. Fred Whitehead lived in the building and his salary was $40 a month. The boathouse displays articles from shipwrecks, with items in the permanent collection dating back to the 1700s.

Location:	301 Southeast MacArthur Boulevard
Hours:	Tuesday through Sunday 11-4, closed major holidays
Fees:	Adults $2, children 6–13 50¢
Phone:	(561) 225-1961 [or 1875]

Hobe Sound

The drive between Hobe Sound and Jupiter along the ocean is particularly beautiful. There is also a lovely small beach at Hobe Sound.

One of Florida's earliest surviving journals was written by Jonathan Dickinson. He, his family, and others were shipwrecked off this coast in the 1690s. They were rescued by Indians at Hobe Sound. Mr. Dickinson, a Quaker, kept a detailed journal of their ordeal entitled *God's Protecting Providence*. It records the fascinating story of their capture, the lives and activities of the Indians, and their eventual release near St. Augustine. Mr. Dickinson and his family continued on to Philadelphia where he published the journal. It became an international best seller and he became a successful merchant and was later elected mayor of Philadelphia.

Florida Indians capturing the shipwreck victims,
drawing done ca. 1707

The highlight of the *Jonathan Dickinson State Park* is the Loxahatchee River, one of the last wild, junglelike waterways in the state. It is the only National Wild and Scenic River in Florida. There are hiking trails and canoe rentals. Consider a 90 minute canoe trip, or a ride on a tour boat up the Loxahatchee River to the

Trapper Nelson Interpretive Site. Try to arrange your visit to listen to the Park Ranger's campfire program on Saturday evening, or take a guided nature walk on Sunday morning. A road near the entrance to the park leads to Hobe Mountain Trail, a 20 minute walk which ends at a tower overlooking the Intracoastal Waterway and Jupiter Island. Climb the tower for a terrific view.

Location:	16450 Southeast Federal Highway
Hours:	**Park:** Daily 8–sunset. **Trapper Nelson Site:** Wednesday through Sunday 9-5. **Campfire Program:** Saturday 7 pm or 8:30 pm DST. **Nature Walk:** Sunday 9 am at the picnic area. **Cruise:** Daily 9,11, 1, and 3
Fees:	**Park:** $3.25 per car, maximum of 8 people per vehicle. $1 per person arriving by foot, bike, bus, or motorcycle. **Cruise:** Adults $10, children $6-12 $5
Phone:	**Park:** (561) 546-2771. **Cruise:** (561) 746-1466

Tequesta

Archaeological evidence shows that Indian tribes lived here more than 2,500 years ago. One of the natural wonders at the site is the largest outcropping of Anastasia limestone on the Atlantic Coast. ***Blowing Rocks Preserve*** is well named. At high tide, whale spouts of water push through the limestone rock and create everchanging natural fountain displays.

Location:	A1A about 3 miles North of Jupiter Inlet
Hours:	Daily 9–5, limited parking
Fees:	No charge

Jupiter

Part of the early history of the southeastern coast of Florida involved the legendary ***Barefoot Mailman***. In the old days, before roads or tourists or railroads or superhighways, it was a challenge to get mail between Jupiter and Miami. The safest and fastest way was to walk the mail down the beach. Beginning in 1870, he walked along the then largely deserted beach and swam or rowed across the inlets. This was one of the more dedicated ways in which the U.S. Post Office maintained its delivery schedule!

Lighthouses are important along the Florida coast. The light at the *Jupiter Inlet Lighthouse and Museum* is visible from 18 miles at sea. Completed in 1860, this is one of the oldest lighthouses on the Atlantic Coast and is the oldest remaining structure in Palm Beach County. Visitors can climb 105 feet for a view of the area. If the day is particularly clear, look for the Gulf Stream which is 15 miles off shore. When you can see it, it looks like a river running through the Atlantic Ocean.

Jupiter Inlet Lighthouse

Location:	US Highway 1 and North Beach Road
Hours:	Sunday through Wednesday 10-4. Last tour leaves at 3:15. Children must be at least four-feet tall to enter the lighthouse
Fees:	$5
Phone:	(561) 747-8380

The shingle-style *Florida History Center and Museum* features the *DuBois Pioneer Home.* The house overlooks Jupiter Inlet. Built by Harry Du Bois for his bride in the late 1890s, it is on the site of the Hobe Indian village where the Jeaga Indians held Jonathan Dickinson and his party captive in 1696. The museum specializes in local history and has several period rooms of antique furniture, clothing and other items belonging to Florida pioneers. The property lies on a 20 foot high, 90 foot long shell mound.

Location:	805 North US Highway 1
Hours:	Tuesday through Friday 10-4, Saturday and Sunday 1-4. **House**: Wednesday and Sunday 1-4
Fees:	**Museum:** Adults $5, Seniors over 55 $4,children 6-12 $3. **DuBois House:** $2
Phone:	(561) 747-6639

Southeastern Florida

We see more contrasts as the trip down Florida's East Coast continues. The next several tours travel from the opulence of Palm Beach to the bustle of Miami, which is one of Florida's international cities. You then go to the deserted wilderness of the Everglades, and finally to Key West at the Southernmost tip of the state, a longtime haven of artists and authors.

Tour 6 notes American opulence. Florida's *Gold Coast* includes the Palm Beach area where mansions line the tour route.

Miami has a rich and varied history. Within Tour 7, *The Miami Seven*—the city's "neighborhoods"—are isolated to show a glimpse of the internationalism and variety of this cosmopolitan city.

Tour 8, *The River of Grass*, leads you into an ecologically critical area, larger than the state of Rhode Island. The Everglades have a rhythm of their own and provide a noted contrast to Miami's urban vibrancy.

Hemingway's Haunts come to life as you drive Tour 9 along the magnificent, waterbound Florida Keys. The tour ends in Key West, a city unlike any other in Florida.

● Palm Beach
● West Palm Beach
● Delray Beach
● Boca Raton
● FT. LAUDERDALE

Tour 6. The Gold Coast

Palm Beach

In 1878 a Spanish barque was wrecked off the shore of what is now Palm Beach. The vessel carried a cargo of coconuts. They were washed ashore and took root. In time the barren sand key was transformed into a beautiful tropical island.

Henry Morrison Flager saw the island and its possibilities in 1893. During this period he was expanding his railroad empire down the coast of Florida and identifying sites for future luxury hotels. He directed the layout of Palm Beach township, built the Royal Poinciana Hotel, and established Palm Beach as a winter retreat for the very, very wealthy. Already a millionaire, he made yet another fortune through his land, railroad, and Florida tourism investments. One example of the opulence of the Gilded Age can be seen at **Whitehall,** the **Henry Morrison Flagler Museum.** This magnificent 55 room mansion was completed in 1902 at a cost of $2.5 million— with an additional $1.5 million spent for furnishings. It was a wedding gift for his third wife.

Mary Lily Kenan Flagler
1902

Whitehall

When it was built, the *New York Herald* called Whitehall the "Taj Mahal of North America." The 60,000 square foot mansion is set in eight acres of grounds bordering Lake Worth. The architecture shows a strong Spanish influence with rooms built around a central courtyard.

Visit Whitehall and learn about the Gilded Age and Henry Flagler's contributions to Florida's development, particularly in railroading, tourism, and agriculture.

Location:	Cocoanut Row at Whitehall Way
Hours:	Tuesday through Saturday 10–5, Sunday 12–5, closed Thanksgiving, Christmas and New Year. Guided tours often available by reservation
Fees:	Adults $7, children 6–12 $3
Phone:	(561) 655–2833

Although Mr. Flagler created Palm Beach, Addison Mizner, architect, prize fighter, and miner, placed his signature upon the town. Many of the Palm Beach Mediterranean–style mansions built during the 1920s were his work. He introduced the Spanish vogue that resulted in a transformation of architecture all along Florida's lower East Coast. His houses were built with courtyards on various levels and had exposed rafters and vaulted ceilings. To obtain the materials needed for these creations, Mr. Mizner established his own factories to manufacture tile, ironwork, furniture, and pottery. He created some of the most beautiful homes in Palm Beach and then moved on to Boca Raton.

It would have been fun to see all the architects who were working in Palm Beach in the 1920s. The ***Breakers***, a landmark hotel of Italian Renaissance design, was built in 1925. It was designed by the New York architectural firm of Schulze and

Weaver, the firm that also designed the Waldorf–Astoria Hotel in New York. One of our favorite ways to explore Palm Beach is to take a long walk *after* enjoying Sunday brunch at the Breakers.

Location:	One South County Road
Phone:	(561) 655-6611

It is a short walk from The Breakers to ***Bethesda–by–the–Sea*** built in 1926. A modified English Gothic–style Episcopal church, its architecture is reminiscent of 15th–century England. In the cloister there are stained glass windows representing the saints of various Christian countries such as St. George of England and St. Joan of France. Stop to see the building and then pause to walk through the adjacent ***Cluett Memorial Garden.***

Location:	141 South County Road
Hours:	Daily 8–5
Fees:	No charge
Phone:	(561) 655–4554

North Palm Beach

Begin your visit to the ***John D. MacArthur Beach State Park*** and the ***William T. Kirby Nature Center*** by watching a short video. Then it's time to play! A nature trail winds through a hardwood hammock. A 1,600 foot boardwalk spans the estuary and leads to the beach and offshore rock reef. A pedestrian bridge leads across a saltwater cove to the beach and there is also an electric tram.

Location:	10900 State Road 703
Hours:	**Park**: Daily sunrise to sunset. **Nature Center**: Wednesday through Monday 9–5
Fees:	**Park**: $3.25 per vehicle for up to 8 people. **Nature Center**: no charge
Phone:	**Park**: (561) 624–6950 **Nature Center**: (561) 624–6952

West Palm Beach

West Palm Beach had its first growth surge in the late 1800s. Its population was made up of the people working on the new Palm Beach hotel, the Royal Poinciana or the Florida East Coast Railroad. In those days, there were no bridges connecting

Palm Beach to West Palm Beach. At Henry Flagler's instruction, all guests, supplies, and day workers were ferried back and forth. He wanted to exclude all visible business enterprise from Palm Beach. As time passed, bridges connected the two communities. However, in many ways, West Palm Beach remains the business center for nearby Palm Beach.

The *Norton Museum of Art* is one of the country's outstanding small museums. It is distinguished by its outstanding permanent collections including French Impressionists, 20th-century American art, Chinese bronzes, and jade, which are housed in the galleries.

Location:	1451 South Olive Avenue
Hours:	Tuesday through Saturday 10–5, Sunday 1–5, closed major holidays
Fees:	Adults $5, students $3
Phone:	(561) 833-2133

The *Ann Norton Sculpture Garden* features the beautiful home and brick sculptures of Ann Norton which are placed within her two and a half acre tropical garden. The sculpture is impressive. The garden also is home to a fine collection of over 200 varieties of palm trees.

Location:	253 Barcelona Road
Hours:	Tuesday through Saturday 10–4
Fees:	No charge, $3 donation requested
Phone:	(561) 832–5328

It is always interesting to look at source documents. Besides historic photographs, if you like architecture visit the *Historical Society of Palm Beach County*. Some of Addison Mizner's architectural drawings and furniture are located here.

Location:	400 North Dixie Highway
Hours:	Tuesday through Friday 10–3
Fees:	Research fee: $5, advance reservation required
Phone:	(561) 832–4164

Travel through an almost–African wildlife environment at African village at *Lion Country Safari*. More than 1,000 animals roam free across the 500 acre preserve. A four mile self guided safari goes through Black Bear Ridge, the Serengeti Plain, Nilgai Forest with elephants and rhinos; and Zebra Hills with giraffes and chimps.

Location:	Southern Boulevard, 18 miles west
Hours:	Daily 9:30–5:30, last car admitted at 4:30. Note: No convertibles admitted, no pets allowed. If you are traveling in a convertible, you can rent a car for $6 per hour
Fees:	Adults $14.95, seniors and children 3–16 $9.95
Phone:	(561) 793–1084

Delray Beach

In 1905, Jo Sakai completed his studies at New York University's School of Commerce. Upon returning to Miyazu, Japan, he organized a pioneering party to settle in what is now Delray Beach. Working with the help of Henry Flagler's Model Land Company, a subsidiary of the Florida East Coast Railroad, Sakai and his companions put a bold economic and social experiment in place—they created a new agricultural community in an almost uninhabited part of Florida.

The group named their community the Yamato Colony. In 1908 a blight killed the pineapple crops. For a time, they grew winter vegetables. When they began raising pineapple again, they realized that Henry Flagler, whose people had worked with them as they created the Colony, had decided to ship Cuban pineapples to Northern markets since he could make a larger profit on them.

By the 1920s, all but one of the colonists had left. George Sukeji Morikami continued to work as a pineapple farmer and agricultural agent in South Florida. He bought land and eventually owned several hundred acres. In the mid–1920s, he gave 200 acres to create a park and museum which would honor the memory of the original Japanese colonists and build a bridge of cultural understanding between his two homelands. It is named the *Morikami Park, Museum, and Japanese Gardens*.

You will leave here with many memories. Stop at the small stone garden with its meditation area. Visit the moat with its manmade waterfall. Note the seven foot Japanese stone lantern honoring Colonel Ellison Onizula, the first Asian–American in space, who was killed in the Challenger space shuttle explosion in 1986. Walk along the one mile nature trail, and look at the Bonsai and Japanese Gardens. Then, after going inside to look at the museum, conclude your visit at the Seishin–An Tea House to observe the traditional art of the tea ceremony.

Location:	4000 Morikami Park Road
Hours:	**Park Grounds:** Daily sunrise to sunset. **Museum:** Tuesday through Sunday 10–5, closed major holidays. **Tea Ceremony:** call ahead for schedule
Fees:	Adults $4.25, seniors over 65 $3.75, children 6–18 $2, Sundays 10–12, no charge
Phone:	(561) 495–0233

Boca Raton

Boca Raton, now a lovely resort and business community, has had several lives. In the 18th– and 19th–centuries it was a terrifying, rough–and–ready pirate's cove. By the early 1920s, architect Addison Mizner traveled down the coast from Palm Beach. He had grand ideas for a luxury resort and built what is now known as the *Boca Raton Hotel and Club*. His Spanish–Gothic–style inn opened in 1925 at a cost of over $1.25 million, making it the most expensive 100 room hotel of its day. Originally, he had planned to have a canal and gondola bringing guests to the hotel. All that remains of that idea today is the stately boulevard.

Location:	501 East Camino Real
Phone:	(561) 395–3000

Unless you're staying at the hotel, one of the most interesting ways to learn about it is to take a guided tour given by the Boca Raton Historical Society. Stop at the *Boca Raton Historical Society Museum,* housed in the original Town Hall to make your tour reservations.

Location:	71 North Federal Highway
Hours:	Museum: Tuesday through Friday 10–4. **Boca Raton Hotel Tours:** Tuesday at 1:30, by appointment only
Fees:	**Museum:** No charge. **Tour:** $5
Phone:	(561) 395–6766

If you're going to be in the area for a few days, visit the ***Boca Raton Chamber of Commerce*** at 1800 North Dixie Highway to pick up their free brochure showing Boca's historic buildings. It is a good architectural reference as you travel around the community.

Tthe ***Boca Raton Museum of Art*** has a fine collection of photography, modern, contemporary, pre–Columbian, and African art. Choose a rainy afternoon and spend it looking at the late 19th– and early 20th–century works by Degas, Matisse, and Picasso.

Location:	801 West Palmetto Park Road
Hours:	Tuesday, Thursday, and Friday 10–4, Wednesday 10–9, Saturday and Sunday 12–4
Fees:	Adults $3, seniors over 65 $2, students with current ID $1, free on Wednesdays
Phone:	(561) 392–2500

In much the same way that earlier millionaires along the East Coast raced automobiles, many of today's millionaires turn to polo, the international sport of kings. If you'd like to see a game, phone the ***Royal Palm Polo Sports Club*** and ask about the schedule. It's a wonderful way to enjoy a winter afternoon watching polo and spectators. Games are held on Wednesday and Sunday afternoons during the season.

A polo match in progress

Location:	18000 Jog Road
Hours:	January through April, phone for schedule
Fees:	**Wednesday**: no charge. **Sunday**: General admission $6, box seats $12
Phone:	(561) 994–1876

Another wonderful way to enjoy an afternoon is to visit the *Gumbo Limbo Nature Center.* Walk along the elevated boardwalk, meander along the nature trail that leads to the Intracoastal Waterway, and climb to the top of the observation tower. Inside, see the aquarium and hands–on exhibits. Then go on to explore the salt water tank, butterfly garden and bird blind. Oh, yes, now that you've been here you'll be able to tell your friends that you've met the mysterious Gumbo Limbo—and don't let them try to tell you it's a new dance step!

Location:	1801 North Ocean Boulevard, Route A1A
Hours:	Monday through Saturday 9-4, Sundays 12-4
Fees:	No charge
Phone:	(561) 338–1473

Fort Lauderdale

Once a hot, steamy mangrove swamp, a U.S. Fort was constructed on the site in 1838 to guard against the Seminole Indians. Named for its commander, Major William Lauderdale, it remained open until 1857. Then all was quiet in the sleepy, shorefront hamlet until Henry Flagler's railroad reached the site in 1911. With the arrival of the steam engine, travel to Fort Lauderdale became easy. Many people worked to capitalize on the real estate opportunities.

Charles Rodes is largely responsible for 20th–century Fort Lauderdale. He studied the parallel canal system used in Venice and transferred the idea to America. There are now more than 300 miles of navigable inland waterways in the Greater Fort Lauderdale area. Impressive homes, imposing docks, and beautiful yachts line many of the canals.

The only home in Florida directly administered by the Florida Trust for Historic Preservation is the *Bonnet House*, built in 1920. It has 30 rooms and was built of native coral stone, Dade

County pine, and concrete blocks poured at the site. Frederic Clay Bartlett was a Chicago art collector and muralist. His first wife, Helen Birch Bartlett, was the daughter of one of Florida's early philanthropists. As a wedding gift, her father gave the couple the 35 acre estate which has 700 feet fronting on the Atlantic Ocean.

The Bartletts decided to build a tropical plantation home. With an open, simple design, it has a two story veranda and rooms wrapping around a large courtyard. The second floor balcony was imported from New Orleans. The studio, the first building on the estate, features a high beamed ceiling, a two story window that admits the northern light, and the Bartlett's art works. When visiting, look closely at the animal murals and carousel carvings. Evelyn, Mr. Bartlett's second wife, was also a painter. Her imagination is clearly evident in the whimsical mood of this landmark site. The house serves as a perfect backdrop for the luxurious exotic gardens they created. Yellow Bonnet water lilies that grow on two small ponds on the property are particularly lovely, and the house is named for them. Arrange to tour this impressive house, the gardens, and the painting studio. It is a wonderful way to look backward to an earlier Fort Lauderdale.

Location:	900 North Birch Road
Hours:	Wednesday through Friday 10-2, Saturday and Sunday 12-3
Fees:	Adults $9, seniors over 60 $8, children 6–18 $7
Phone:	(954) 563–5393

Time for another just–for–children stop. The **Museum of Discovery and Science** is a hands–on science, art, and history facility. For starters, go cave crawling, bend light rays, and see the Space Base exhibit which simulates a short space flight.

Location:	401 Southwest Second Street
Hours:	**Museum**: Monday through Saturday 10–5, Sunday 12–6, closed Christmas. **IMAX:** hours are extensive and vary
Fees:	**Museum:** Adults $6, seniors over 65 and children 3–12 $5. **IMAX:** Adults $9, seniors over 65 $8, children 3-12 $7
Phone:	(954) 467-6637

If you care about competitive swimming, diving, water

polo, synchronized swimming and water safety, the ***International Swimming Hall of Fame Aquatic Complex –Museum and Pool*** is the place to see. There are movies so you can watch Olympic highlights of swimming, diving, water polo, and synchronized swimming. There are medals, trophies, and action exhibits highlighting the accomplishments of more than 300 aquatic greats from over 100 countries. And don't forget to bring your bathing suit. After looking at the greats, it's always fun to see how much our style and speed improves in these championship pools!

Location:	One Hall of Fame Drive
Hours:	**Museum:** Daily 9–7. **Art Gallery:** Monday through Friday 9-5. **Pool**: Daily 8–4 and also on Monday through Friday from 6-8 pm. Closed during swim meets
Fees:	**Museum and Art Gallery**: Family $5, Adults $3, seniors over 65, military personnel and children 7–12 $1. **Pool:** Adults $3, seniors, military personnel, and students $2
Phone:	**Museum and Art Gallery:** (954) 462–6536 **Pool**: (954) 468-1580

One of the largest collections of ethnographic material in Florida is housed at the fan–shaped ***Museum of Art***. The collection includes Oceanic, West African, pre–Columbian, and American Indian art. The CoBrA Collection, featuring postwar art from Copenhagen, Brussels, and Amsterdam, is always interesting to see as is a pleasant pause at the sculpture terrace.

Location:	One East Las Olas Boulevard
Hours:	Tuesday through Thursday and Saturday 10–5, Friday 10-8, Sunday 1–5, closed major holidays
Fees:	Adults $6, seniors over 65 $5, students over 12 $3 children 8-12 $1
Phone:	(954) 525–5500

Stranahan House, built in 1901, is the oldest home on its original site in Broward County. Originally it was a trading post for Seminole Indians from the Everglades. The building has been restored to show how it looked in the 1913–1915 era, providing an interesting glimpse of how people lived in early Fort Lauderdale.

Location:	335 Southeast Sixth Avenue
Hours:	Wednesday through Saturday 10–4, Sunday 1–4,

	closed major holidays
Fees:	Adults $5, children under 12 $2
Phone:	(954) 524–4736

See a replica of the city's first school house at the *Florida Historical Museum.* The museum shows local artifacts from the first permanent settlement in the 1890s, the Seminole War period, and more recent items. Of particular interest is the large collection of period photographs.

Location:	219 Southwest Second Avenue
Hours:	Tuesday through Friday 10–4
Fees:	Adults $2, students $1
Phone:	(954) 463–4431

Coconut Creek

Just a few miles inland in Coconut Creek is *Butterfly World.* A screened–in tropical rain forest houses over 150 species of colorful butterflies. Visit during the afternoon when they are most active. A must–see stop! Visitors stroll through three acres of beautiful, lush, tropical gardens while thousands of live, brilliantly colored butterflies soar around them. Waterfalls, fish, birds, orchids and roses complete the natural habitat. A butterfly farm, botanical gardens, museum/insectarium, gift and plant shops, and outdoor cafe are also on the premises.

This was the world's first butterfly house with over 150 species of live butterflies. Bring your camera. The Tropical Rain Forest has butterflies from Central and South America. North American butterflies can be seen in one aviary, those from around the world in another. The hummingbirds are always wonderful to watch and children enjoy traveling across the suspension bridge.

Location:	3600 West Sample Road in Tradewinds Park South
Hours:	Monday through Saturday 9–5, Sunday 1–5. Admission gate closes at 4 pm daily.
Fees:	Adults $10.95, children 4–12 $6
Phone:	(954) 977–4434

The magnificent Art Deco District,
Miami Beach

Tour 7.
The
Miami
Seven

Seven metropolitan Miami communities are highlighted as part of this tour. Each area has a different personality. When you have completed the trip you will have a better understanding of the city's cosmopolitan, international nature.

One cautionary comment should be made. Miami can be a difficult city for tourists. Watch your belongings, realize you're in a large, metropolitan, multinational, multicultural city, and act accordingly.

Miami

Long, long ago a shipwrecked sailor was saved by the Tequesta Indians and lived among them near Lake Okeechobee. The Indians named the place the *Lake of Mayaime* which was shortened to Miami, Tequestan for "sweet water."

What changes have happened since that shipwrecked sailor landed! European settlement began, the harbor area became a Spanish stronghold, and an American fort was built to protect the early settlers from the Indians. By the late 1800s, Miami had become a small, quiet fishing village. Transportation to other parts of Florida was slow and difficult. There were no overland roads and most settlers came by sea. There were almost no tourists. As we noted earlier, even getting mail through from Jupiter was a challenging experience.

Then came a few hearty Northerners seeking the mild winter climate. Miami's 20th–century evolution was about to begin. Julia Tuttle, a displaced Clevelander, understood Miami's potential. She single–handedly became the city's greatest pro-moter. Julia Tuttle knew what Henry Flagler and his Florida East

Julia Tuttle

Coast Railroad were doing far-ther up the coast. Since she owned land in Miami, she knew a rail-road would help her city grow. She wrote to Henry Flagler in glowing terms about the area's warm winter weather. She at-tached a few branches of orange blossoms and we assume that the Barefoot Mailman carried the blossoms and her note urging Mr. Flagler to extend his railroad all the way to Miami. She and the sweetly scented orange blossoms convinced him to do just that.

Henry Flagler's expansion of the railroad and his hotel building brought other developers to the growing city. It soon became a winter resort attracting visitors and residents from all over the country and the world. Over the decades, an influx of Latin Americans began. This was partially prompted by political unrest in several Caribbean and South American countries, increasing from the 1960s with the migration of the Cubans. Miami is now a melting pot of Caribbean, Central, North, and South American cultures.

An interesting first stop to begin to understand the diver-sity of the area is *The Historical Museum of Southern Florida and the Caribbean.* It houses a large collection of artifacts and documents that focus on the cultural and social history of South Florida, the region extending from Lake Okeechobee to Key West. Exhibits include a Spanish fort, Indian Chickee huts, and a restored 19th–century Miami trolley. Be sure to see the Tropical Dreams exhibit showing Cuban presence in Southern Florida. The *Charlton W. Tebeau Research Library of Florida History* has magnificent historical photographs and many documents which preserve Cu-ban heritage in Florida.

Location:	Miami–Dade Cultural Center, 101 West Flagler Street
Hours:	**Museum:** Monday through Saturday 10–5, Thursday 10–9, Sunday 12–5. **Tebeau Research Library:** Monday through Friday 10-4:30, closed Thanksgiving, Christmas and New Years Day
Fees:	Adults $4, seniors over 62 $3, children 6–12 $2 Mondays no charge, donations welcome
Phone:	(305) 375–1492

The Miami Art Museum is dedicated solely to the display of international art from World War II to the present. Recent acquisitions include works by Louise Nevelson, Robert Rauschenberg, James Rosenquist, and Helen Frankenthaler.

Location:	Miami–Dade Cultural Center, 101 West Flagler
Hours:	Tuesday, Wednesday, and Friday 10-5, Thursday 10-9, Saturday and Sunday 12-5
Fees:	Adults $5, seniors over 65 and students with ID $2.50. Tuesday contribution of the visitor's choice, Thursday 5-9 no charge
Phone:	(305) 375–3000

In 1925 an ornate Mediterranean–style building was erected for Paramount Studios. Now known as the *Gusman Center for the Performing Arts,* it remains ornate. Step inside and enjoy the view—and perhaps a performance!

Location:	174 East Flagler Street
Phone:	(305) 374–2444

It's hard to think of the opulence of the rich in the early days of the 20th-century. Difficult, that is, until one visits *Vizcaya Museum and Gardens*. James Deering, a Chicago industrialist and Vice President of International Harvester, wanted to create a special winter retreat. After much deliberation with architects, art dealers, and art historians, building began. His home was completed in 1916.

This is one of Florida's grandest homes, an elaborate Italian Renaissance palazzo–style mansion overlooking Biscayne Bay. The villa may be approached through a 10 acre formal garden recreating a 17th–century Italian hill garden with plantings, gazebos, pools, grottoes, mazes, sculpture, cascades and fountains. It took 1,000 workers (then 10% of Miami's population) two years to build the $15 million mansion. The walls are stone and stucco. Today, 34 of the 70 halls and rooms are open to the public and are filled with magnificent works of art and furnishings. It is opulent. It should be pointed out that James Deering was a bachelor and lived in the palazzo until his death in 1925. Vizcaya grew to become his personal celebration of the European decorative arts, with the museum representing the Renaissance, Baroque, Rococo, and Neoclassic periods.

The gardens were designed to reflect the elegance of the Renaissance and Baroque periods. They invite contemplation and reflection. Close your eyes to fully experience the unique textures, smells, and sounds.

Location:	3251 South Miami Avenue
Hours:	Daily 9:30–5:00, last admission1/2 hour before closing time. Closed Christmas
Fees:	Adults $10, children 6–12 $5
Phone:	(305) 250–9133

Children can learn about light, sound, electronics, biology, and energy at the *Miami Museum of Science* and the *Space Transit Planetarium.* The facility has well over 100 hands–on exhibits. The Wildlife Center features live giant insects, reptiles, and marine life. The Coral Reef exhibit is exceptional. The Body in Action exhibit and the computer labs are fun to see as is the walk–in aviary. Play virtual reality basketball or log on to a web site, or use CD-ROMs. On clear nights, sky viewing through the telescope on the roof of the Weintraub Observatory is wonderful.

Location:	3280 South Miami Avenue
Hours:	**Museum and Planetarium:** Daily 10–6, closed Thanksgiving and Christmas. **Observatory:** Saturday 8–10:30, weather permitting. Observatory star show: First Saturday of each month at 7 pm. **Laser Shows:** Friday and Saturday, 8:30, 9:30, 10:45, and midnight
Fees:	**Museum, Planetarium, and Observatory:** Adults $9, seniors over 62 and students $7, children 3-12 $5.50. **Laser Show:** Adults $6, children 3–12 $3.
Phone:	**Museum:** (305) 854–4247. **Planetarium:** (305) 854-4242

When you need an oasis in the midst of the busy city, visit the *Mildred and Claude Pepper Bayfront Park.* It combines monuments and spaces for quiet reflection and was designed by Isamo Noguchi. Walk through the park and pause to honor such international heroes as Christopher Columbus and José Cecello del Valle, who wrote Honduras' Federal Constitution. Look for the John F. Kennedy Memorial Torch of Friendship symbolizing friendship between Miami and Latin American countries. The park is also the site of the Challenger Space Shuttle Memorial. The Liberty Column is a monument to the Cuban rafters and pays homage to the thousands of unknown rafters lost at sea.

Location:	301 Biscayne Boulevard
Hours:	Monday through Friday 9-5
Phone:	(305) 358–7550

Bayside, at the foot of Biscayne Boulevard, is a nearby area of colorful shops, restaurants, and entertainment on an outdoor stage. This is an interesting spot to pause to enjoy the pink plaza and the waterfront.

Sailboats in the harbor

Speaking of the waterfront, there is simply no place like the *Port of Miami.* Bring binoculars and an atlas to help you recognize the home port of each magnificent passenger liner you will see docked at this port, the largest cruise passenger facility in the world. Watch the efficiency with which the passengers, luggage, and thousands of items that make trips enjoyable are loaded onto the giant liners.

Location:	One–half mile east of Biscayne Boulevard

For many new Miami residents, the ***Freedom Tower*** at 600 Biscayne Boulevard is the equivalent of an earlier generation's Statue of Liberty. Modeled after the Giralda Tower in Seville, Spain, it was built in 1925 and is reflective of Spanish Renaissance Revival architecture. The building housed the ***Miami Daily News*** for years. In 1962, it was renamed in honor of Cuban refugees since nearly half a million of them were processed through this gateway to the United States. The tower served as a reception center for Cuban refugees who arrived in Miami between 1962 and 1974.

The ***American Police Museum and Hall of Fame*** has over 10,000 items on display and is a fascinating stop for those who are seriously interested in law enforcement. There is also a Memorial honoring the U.S. Police Officers who lost their lives in the line of duty. Don't leave without seeing the Crime Scene where you can test your own detective skills.

Location:	3801 Biscayne Boulevard
Hours:	Daily 10–5:30, closed Christmas
Fees:	Adults $6, seniors over 62 $4, children $3, out–of–state police officers $1, Florida peace officers and family survivors, no charge
Phone:	(305) 573–0700

For an unusual musical experience, pause at the ***Miami Marine Stadium***. Located at 3601 Rickenbacker Causeway, it was designed to meet its audience on land and sea! Watch and hear a concert from the grandstand in the traditional way or watch and listen from your boat. Views and sound are excellent from both locations. Watch local newspapers for show information and make your reservation early.

The ***Miami Seaquarium*** describes marine mammals through shows and exhibits featuring a killer whale, dolphins, sea lions, and manatees. Watch for the large fish swimming in the main tank which has two viewing levels. Sharks swim freely in a channel. It's always interesting to watch them. We also enjoy the large reef aquarium. This is a wonderful place to get a close–up look at sealife—without getting wet.

Location:	4400 Rickenbacker Causeway
Hours:	Daily 9:30–6, last admission 90 minutes before closing
Fees:	Adults $19.95, children 3–9 $14.95
Phone:	(305) 361–5705

Little Havana is Miami's Latin Quarter and Calle Ocho is its main street. Drive along Calle Ocho until you find your stop for a cup of strong Cuban coffee. Plan to take home a loaf of Cuban bread, do some shopping, and appreciate the diversity of the city. The area is growing. It is currently a roughly 30 block strip on Southwest Eighth Street, also called Calle Ocho, boundaried by Flagler Street.

There are five major markers in the ***Cuban Memorial Plaza*** at Memorial Boulevard and Eighth Street. There is a bronze bust of General Antonio Maceo, an Afro–Cuban general who led troops in the 1895 Cuban War for Independence. Known as the "Bronze Titan," his courage and love of country are memorialized. A bronze map of Cuba is dedicated to the "ideals of people who will never forget the pledge of making their fatherland free." A statue of the Virgin Mary represents the Cuban family's reverence of motherhood and devotion to the Virgin Mary. There is a statue of Nestor A. "Tony" Izquierdo, a Cuban revolutionary hero who fought in the Bay of Pigs Invasion. It is dedicated to the Martyrs of the Assault of April 17, 1961. Be sure to note the Eternal Torch in Honor of the 2506 Brigade, a memorial to the men who died in the 1961 Bay of Pigs Invasion of Cuba. It should be noted that Cuban born sculptor Tony López created the Izquierdo and Maceo pieces.

The ***Cuban Museum of the Americas*** is dedicated to the preservation of Cuba's pre–revolutionary cultural heritage. There are exhibits of traditional and contemporary Hispanic artists living outside of Cuba, historical documents, and memorabilia. Be sure to note the 1895 Cuban flag. The museum also has a large collection of works by Cuban masters.

Location:	1300 Southwest 12th Avenue
Hours:	Tuesday through Friday 12-6
Fees:	No charge, suggested donation adults $3, students $1
Phone:	(305) 858–8006

71

Days filled with sightseeing could easily be spent in Miami. However, it is now time to move on to Miami Beach, the second of the Miami Seven.

Miami Beach

Carl Fisher, a masterful developer, made Miami Beach his city. He understood the development opportunity that would occur if he converted what was a sandspit into an international resort. Mr. Fisher was a master promoter. In 1919, he used elephants to 'elephant–doze' a new city, Miami Beach, into being from the mangrove sandspur.

The Art Deco District stretches from sixth to 23rd Streets. It contains more than 70 blocks with over 800 buildings, built from the 1920s to the 1940s, designed in the Art Deco style. In one sense, these buildings are large–scale sculptures. In total, they represent the largest remaining collection of Art Moderne/Art Deco structures in America. Tours are available through the *Miami Beach Historic Architectural District's Welcome Center* and are highly recommended. This area is the only National Historic District which has been built in the 20th century. Ocean Drive, between Sixth and 13th Streets, comes alive each evening with outdoor cafes and music from many eras and cultures.

Location:	**Welcome Center:** 1001 Ocean Drive
Hours:	**Walking Tours:** Thursday at 6:30 pm, Saturday at 10:30 am. **Bike Tours:** Every first and third Sunday at 10:30 am
Fees:	**Walking Tours:** $10 per person. **Bike Tours:** $10 per person plus $5 bike rental
Phone:	(305) 672–2014

The *Bass Museum of Art* is noted for its Oriental bronzes as well as its 14th– to 20th–century European paintings, sculpture, textiles, and decorative arts. If your time is limited, go right to the rare collection of 16th–century tapestries and the sculpture dating back to the Middle Ages. They are exceptional.

Location:	2121 Park Avenue
Hours:	Tuesday through Saturday 10–5, Sunday 1–5 and second and fourth Wednesdays 1–9, closed holidays

Fees: Adults $5, seniors and students $3
Phone: (305) 673–7530

To learn more about the Jewish experience in Florida from 1763 to the present, visit the ***Jewish Museum of Florida (Sanford Ziff): Home of MOSAIC***. The building is located in a restored 1936 synagogue. It has a Moorish copper dome and 80 stained glass windows and is in the historic South Beach Art Deco District.

Location: 301 Washington Avenue
Hours: Tuesday through Sunday 10–5. Closed major
                 Jewish holidays
Fees: Adults $5, seniors over 55 and students $4,
                 family $10
Phone: (305) 672–5044

Also located in the historic Art Deco District, plan to see the decorative, design, and architectural arts collections at the ***Wolfsonian.***

Location: 1001 Washington Avenue
Hours: Tuesday and Wednesday through Saturday 11-6,
                 Thursday 11-9, Sunday 12-5
Fees: Adults $5, seniors and students over 6 $3.50.
                 Thursday 6-9 no charge, donations welcome
Phone: (305) 531-1001

North Miami Beach

Be prepared. The next stop is beyond all expectation. You are about to visit the oldest reconstructed building in the western hemisphere. It was built for Spanish King Alphonso VII, 12th–century royalty, to commemorate his defeat of the Moors. The building was originally erected in 1141. It is the oldest building in this hemisphere. The ***Ancient Spanish Monastery of St. Bernard de Clairvaux Cloisters*** was built by slaves. Look carefully and you can see the stonemason's symbols carved into the rock in the 12th–century. The Star of David was used by Jewish slave workers, the Crescent shape was carved by Moorish slaves, and a Cross was carved by Christian slaves. The word awesome comes to mind.

The story of the Monastery and Cloisters' arrival in North Miami bears telling. We've already discussed some of the opulent mansions built in Florida. Throughout the state there are museums filled with amazing the results of European shopping excursions for art, tapestries, rooms, and buildings. This may have been the most unusual purchase. William Randolph Hearst, a California millionaire, never had a home in Florida. However, like very wealthy Floridians, he often went shopping in Europe for important additions to San Simeon, his California estate. He saw the **Monastery of St. Bernard** in Spain and purchased it as it stood. It was carefully dismantled, stone by stone, and packed in straw.

Unfortunately, or perhaps fortunately for us, the stones were not numbered during dismantling. The only numbering done was to identify the order in which the 10,751 crates were to be reassembled. When the crates arrived at U.S. Customs, a serious problem came to light. Because of an epidemic of hoof and mouth disease in Spain, the crates were held in quarantine in New York. The stones could come in, but not the straw. Each crate would have to be opened, each stone taken out. The straw would have to be destroyed. And, only then, could the stones be reloaded into the crates. Mr. Hearst lost interest in the project and did not accept the shipment. The magnificent structure stayed in crates in a warehouse in Brooklyn until he died in 1951. The ancient monastery was not claimed. Finally, several Florida men purchased the crates. It took 23 men three months to carefully unpack them. It took another 19 months and $1.5 million to put the buildings together. A decade later, Colonel Robert Pentland purchased the Cloisters and gave them to the diocese for use as a parish church.

If you visit only one church building in Florida, this would be my recommendation. The chapter house, a room with vaulted ceilings, was once the site of the Recitation of Chapters from the Rule of Benedict. A baptismal font, now used for parish baptisms, dates to the original church as does a life–sized statue of Alphonso VII, the king who ordered construction of the monastery after his successful defeat of the Moors in battle. Services are held in the small chapel, originally the monastery's dining hall, on Sundays and Wednesdays.

Location:	16711 West Dixie Highway
Hours:	Monday through Saturday 10–4, Sunday 12–4, closed major holidays

Fees: Adults $4. 50, seniors over 65 $2.50, children under
                  12 $1
Phone: (305) 945–1461

At Florida International University there is an important reference facility, the **Holocaust Documentation and Education Center**. The center records and maintain testimonies of survivors, liberators, and rescuers.

Location: 300 Northeast 145th Street at Florida International
                  University, North Campus
Hours: Monday through Friday 9–5, closed national and
                  Jewish holidays
Fees: No charge
Phone: (305) 919–5690

Take a walk at **Arch Creek Park.** The natural limestone bridge forms an arch over the North Miami Creek. There is a midden with shell remnants from a prehistoric Indian refuse heap and a small museum of archaeological artifacts. The nature walk shows the history of the Tequesta Indians. Be sure to see the butterfly garden.

Location: 1855 Northeast 135th Street
Hours: Daily 9-5
Fees: No charge
Phone: (305) 944–6111

Since 1980, Haitians have settled in large numbers in an area now called **Little Haiti,** once known as Lemon City. Be sure to see the Caribbean Market at Northeast Second Avenue and Northeast 59th Street. Its terrace was modeled after the Iron Market in Port au Price and has a Caribbean feel. The area is roughly boundaried by Northeast 46th Street to 79th Street between Miami Avenue and Northeast Second Avenue.

Key Biscayne

Bill Baggs Cape Florida State Recreation Area is exceptional. Begin at the **Cape Florida Lighthouse**, built about 1825. it was another in the line of safety nets along the Eastern Coast. In 1836, Seminole Indians trapped the keeper and his assistant in the tower and tried to burn the lighthouse down. The lighthouse keeper threw a keg of explosives from the top of the building and frightened them away. The explosion was heard by a passing patrol ship and the keeper and his assistant were rescued. This may be one of the few cases on record where a boat's crew saved a lighthouse and its keeper. The restored lighthouse keeper's quarters looks much like it did in the 1830s. The recreation area is named for Bill Baggs, a former editor of the *Miami Herald*.

Location:	1200 South Crandon Boulevard, off Rickenbacker
Hours:	Daily 8–sunset
Fees:	**Park:** $4 per vehicle, maximum of 8 people per car
Phone:	(305) 361–5811

Coconut Grove

Coconut Grove began as a winter resort in the late 1800s. Commodore Ralph Middleton Monroe, a photographer, naval architect, and builder of shallow draft boats, was largely responsible for Coconut Grove's emergence as an artistic and cultural center. In 1882, he encouraged Charles and Isabella Peacock to build the first hotel on the South Florida mainland. The Grove, as the area became known, developed into a spirited, diversified community. It attracted New England intellectuals, Key West Conchs, Bahamians, year–round residents, and winter visitors.

Commodore Monroe named his home the Barnacles. It now serves as the centerpiece of the *Barnacle State Historic Site* providing a fine introduction to how the area looked before Miami's large–scale development occurred in the 1920s and 1930s. Since Commodore Monroe built boats, he was particularly interested in the efficient use of space. As you tour the house, notice the practicality of how he designed the furniture and fittings. We especially recommend a look at the boathouse!

Location:	3485 Main Highway
Hours:	**Grounds:** Friday through Sunday 9–4. **House Tour:** Friday through Sunday 10, 11:30, 1:30, and 2:30. Be sure to sign up for the tours at the front porch as soon as you arrive since only ten people can be admitted on each tour. Closed major holidays.
Fees:	**Park:** $1. **Tour:** no charge
Phone:	(305) 448–9445 or (305) 723–8303

Probably the finest example of Spanish Mission church architecture can be seen at the **Plymouth Congregational Church**, built in 1895. Be sure to note the belfry towers and small cloister. The door is over 400 years old and was once the entrance to a small Spanish monastery in the Pyrenees.

Location:	3429 Devon Road
Hours:	Weekdays 8:30-4:30 or Sunday service at 10:30
Phone:	(305) 444–6521

Coral Gables

Coral Gables is an early example of a planned community. It was founded in the 1920s and is widely considered the oldest planned community in the U.S. Everything was done in Spanish style, including elaborate entrances, fountains, and plazas. Most of the streets are named after places in Spain. Stop at the Chamber of Commerce at 50 Aragon Avenue for a self guided tour map. Then take a leisurely bike ride to appreciate George Merrick's genius as a master community planner. Within the 12 mile square city, George Merrick incorporated a Mediterranean community, a walled–in South African compound, and a section of Dutch– and Chinese–inspired residences. The results are interesting and imaginative, particularly since he never visited any of these countries.

When Mr. Merrick began designing his new town, there was a large, somewhat ugly, limestone quarry just where he wanted to place the entrance to the community. He finally found a perfect solution: a **Venetian Pool.** With the large tropical pool and attached Venetian building, he solved his design problem. A beautiful and ornate entrance to the community occurred and a recreational facility was created.

Location:	2701 DeSoto Boulevard

George Merrick's boyhood home is now the **Coral Gables Merrick House**. Its original 1898 board and batten construction remains, as does the 1906 addition of locally quarried fossil–bearing limestone. Designed by George's mother, Althea, it is a fine adaptation of a New England design transitioned into a plantation home using local Florida building materials. It has been restored to represent Coral Gables architecture and room settings as they would have been at the turn of the century. The adjacent botanical garden is also well well worth a visit.

Location:	907 Coral Way
Hours:	**House:** Wednesday and Sunday 1–4 and by appointment. **Garden:** Daily sunrise to sunset, closed Easter and Christmas
Fees:	**House:** Adults $2, children 50¢. **Garden:** no charge
Phone:	(305) 460-5361

The *Biltmore Hotel* was completed in 1926 and renovated in 1986. There are 25 foot high ceilings with frescoes, an oak paneled reception area, and a 300 foot bell tower in this Moorish–style hotel. It is a good example of the opulence wealthy tourists expected in the 1920s.

Location:	1200 Anastasia Avenue
Hours:	**Tours:** Sunday 1:30, 2:30 and 3:30
Fees:	No charge
Phone:	(305) 445–1926

Stop at the *City Hall*, built between 1927–1928. It is a good example of Mr. Merrick's interpretation of Mediterranean revival architecture.

Location:	405 Biltmore Way

Another architectural gem is the *Coral Gables Congregational Church.* It was the city's first church and has a Mediterranean revival design with barrel tiles and ornate baroque ornaments. Note the bell tower. Inside, there are 16th–century furnishings and beautiful pews carved from native pecky cypress.

Location:	3010 DeSoto Boulevard
Hours:	Monday through Friday 8:30-4:30. Call ahead.
Fees:	No charge, donations welcome
Phone:	(305) 448–7421

The *Lowe Art Museum* houses the Kress Italian Renaissance and Baroque art and furniture collections, the Cintas Foundation's Spanish master paintings, and art of Asia. Be sure to see the El Grecos while you're there.

Location:	1301 Stanford Drive on the University of Miami campus
Hours:	Tuesday, Wednesday, Friday and Saturday 10–5, Thursday 12-7, Sunday 12–5, closed major holidays
Fees:	Adults $5, seniors over 65 and students $3
Phone:	(305) 284–3535

We all take hurricanes seriously in southern Florida. Learn about them at the *National Hurricane Center.* We can't recommend this visit more highly. Be better prepared by spending an hour learning about the important work being done at the Center and learning about what you should do to protect your home and family.

Location:	11691 Southwest 17th Street
Hours:	**Tours:** December 1 to May 15, Tuesdays and Thursdays at 11 and 1
Fees:	No charge
Phone:	(305) 229-4470

Opened in 1938, the *Fairchild Tropical Garden* is one of the largest botanical gardens in the continental U.S. Plan a leisurely visit. There are over 80 acres of gardens for viewing. Look inside the rare plant house, walk through the rain forest, and see the sunken garden. There is a 40 minute guided tram tour as well as a self guided walking tour. Whether you're a serious botanist, or simply interested in a beautiful stroll, you're sure to find a wonderful variety of rare plants that you've never seen before.

Location:	10901 Old Cutler Road
Hours:	Daily 9:30–4:30, closed Christmas
Fees:	Adults $8, including tram tour
Phone:	(305) 667–1651

South Miami

The *Miami Metrozoo* is a 290 acre facility. It provides visitors the opportunity to see exotic animals from Africa, Asia, and Europe in environments similar to their natural habitats. There are animal shows daily—try to arrange your visit to see at least one of them. The zoo is one of only a few in the U.S. featuring a prominent koala exhibit. Another highlight is the African Plains section. Be sure to see the rare white Bengal tigers prowling in front

of a replica of a 13th–century Cambodian temple, Children especially enjoy the Children's Zoo.

Location:	12400 Southwest 152nd Street
Hours:	Daily 9:30-5:30, last admission at 4 pm.
Fees:	Adults $8, children 3–12 $4
Phone:	(305) 251–0401

After you think you've done everything at the zoo, there
is more. If you're a railroad buff, you're in for a treat. The *Gold
Coast Railroad Museum* includes a collection of antique trains.
The Ferdinand Magellan Pullman car was built in 1928. It was one
of the last private railcars built. In 1942 it was outfitted with
bulletproof glass, steel plating, and escape hatches for President
Franklin D. Roosevelt's use. He liked to travel at about 35 miles per
hour. Harry Truman used the Magellan for a 21,000 mile whistlestop
campaign in 1948 and moved at much faster speeds! In 1984,
President Ronald Reagan used the car. At that time, the Presiden-
tial seal that you see was added. And that's part of the story of only
one of the trains you'll see here.

Location:	12450 Southwest 152nd Street
Hours:	Monday through Friday 11-3, Saturday and Sunday 11-4
Fees:	Adults $5, children 3–12 $2
Phone:	(305) 253–0063

One of our favorite jungle settings is *Parrot Jungle and
Gardens.* It has an extensive collection of parrots and exotic birds.
Arrange your day so you can see the wildlife shows, the Creature
in the Mist, and the tropical gardens.

Location:	11000 Southwest 57th Avenue
Hours:	Daily 9:30–6, last admission at 5
Fees:	Adults $12.95, seniors over 62 $11.65, children 3–10 $8.95
Phone:	(305) 666–7834

Homestead O
Florida City O

Tour 8.
River
of
Grass

The River of Grass Tour provides the opportunity to observe and learn about nature and yourself. Before beginning the trip, read *The Everglades, River of Grass*, by Marjory Stoneman Douglas. She shares her comments and concerns about the importance of the natural environment. Her work serves as an important example of how to help insure the continuation of this national treasure. Within the *Everglades National Park* it is easy to forget time when observing migratory birds, the ever changing river of grass, and the natural environment. The next stop leads underwater where the immensity of the natural environment and the importance of preserving it persists. The *Biscayne National Underwater Park* is an exceptionally beautiful environment for observing underseas creatures.

Be careful. The River of Grass Tour is not for the casual visitor. The mystery and beauty of what you experience will be with you forever.

Homestead

Homestead was developed by Henry Flagler to provide housing for his employees and their families as the Miami to Key West portion of the East Coast Railroad was being built.

During the 1930s, there was a great deal of concern for the preservation of the Everglades, one of Florida's natural wonders. In 1934, Congress accepted the state's proposal and over 2,000 square miles of land were set aside. In 1947 when the *Everglades National Park* was finally created, the area was set at 1,400,533 acres. Of this acreage, about half is land, half is water.

The Everglades is the largest remaining subtropical wilderness in the country. Although comparatives can be discussed, the key to the Everglades is its constantly changing nature. At its core, the Everglades is a slowly moving freshwater river of grass. It is over 50– miles wide and only inches deep, flowing about 100 miles from Lake Okeechobee to the southern tip of the Florida peninsula. As you travel, watch for birds and wildlife. The sky's changing patterns and reflections serve as the backdrop to this magnificent natural environment.

The Everglades, a river of grass, 1952

Watch for signs to the Flamingo Visitor Center, the best known entrance to the ***Everglades National Park***. The Visitor Center at the park entrance and the Royal Palm Visitor Center along Anhinga Trail are well worth seeing. From the Royal Palm Center, there is a half mile boardwalk over wetlands and ponds. Look for alligators, snakes, and birds. Another trail, the Gumbo Limbo Trail has tropical trees and plants. About 14 miles farther inside the park, the Pa–hay–okee Trail leads about a quarter mile to an observation tower. The Mahogany Hammock Trail is about 21 miles from the entrance and at the 25 mile point, Paurotis Pond has a canoe trail. No canoes to rent, so bring your own. Nine Mile Pond Canoe Trail is 28 miles from the entrance and West Lake canoe trail is 32 miles from the entrance. Once again, we empha-size that this is wilderness territory. Particularly if you plan to canoe, be sure to discuss your trip with the Park Ranger. While there, attend one of the Park Ranger talks. Then take a tram or a sightseeing boat trip. Realizing that this is Florida, be prepared for storms, mosquitoes, high humidity, and possibly a hurricane, particularly if you travel during the summer months. Your visit will be enhanced by bringing along birding, tree, and tropical plant identification books—and don't forget your binoculars. We particularly recommend the Boat Tour which leaves from the Park Ranger Station. Since there are a few entrances to the park, ask the most direct route to the station when you first arrive. This is a safe and extraordinary way to understand the ecological importance of the Everglades. Another wonderful trip is the Shark Valley Tram Tour which travels through the ultrasharp sawgrass and wilderness.

Be alert as you travel and stay on the marked routes. There are boardwalks over swampy areas and blacktopped trails. The wildlife here is to be taken very, very seriously. Each experience in the Everglades is different. Come with a sense of peacefulness and a readiness to learn. You won't be disappointed.

Location:	40001 State Route 9336, 12 miles southwest of Homestead. **Boat Tours:** Departs from the Visitor Center at Everglades City and/or the Marina at Flamingo. **Tram Tour:** Departs from the Park Office off Route 41
Hours:	**Visitor Centers** : Daily 8–5. **Boat Tours**: Daily 8:30–5. **Tram Tours:** October through April 9–3, balance of year as weather permits
Fees:	**Park:** $10 per vehicle, including riders. $5 per person entering on foot, bicycle, bus, etc. **Boat Tour:** Back Country Boat Tour: Adults $16, children $8. Florida Bay Boat Tour: Adults $10, children $5. **Tram Tours:** Adults $8, advance reservations suggested for boat and tram tours
Phone:	**Flamingo Visitor Center:** (305) 242–7700.

Located in the Everglades, the *Chekika State Recreation Area* has over 100 species of birds, alligators, and otters. When the water table becomes low, be on the lookout for the rare, endangered Florida panther.

Back in 1839 to 1840, during the Second Seminole Indian Wars, U.S. Army soldiers set out in 16 canoes to find Chief Chekika's hideaway. It was believed that Chekika had been responsible for several attacks on settlers in the area. The soldiers paddled down Everglades waterways, surprised and killed him. The Chekika Raid marked the first time the U.S. Army moved into an inaccessible area to wage a battle.

For a present–day visit, bring a bathing suit to step into the cool sulphur water from the artesian well that forms a waterfall into Lake Chekika where more than three million gallons flow daily. There is also an interpretive center with an Everglades exhibit.

Location:	168th Street and Southwest 237th Avenue
Hours:	Daily 8-6
Fees:	$8 per private vehicle or $4 per person walking or biking
Phone:	(305) 251-0371

One of the difficulties when describing national treasures is to avoid using too many superlatives. So, let it simply be said that the *Biscayne National Underwater Park* is magnificent! There are more than 180,000 acres of islands and reefs to explore. With less than 5% of the park out of the water, bring scuba gear or snorkeling equipment. Of particular interest is the *Offshore Reefs Archaeological District*, where hard and soft coral extend for more than 30 miles in a north–south direction and four to seven miles in an east–west direction.

While at the Park, there is always the possibility of locating a treasure from one of the over 40 shipwrecks in the area. Scuba diving and snorkeling equipment can be rented. Even if you are not interested in being in the water, the glass–bottomed boat tour should be experienced.

Location:	**For tours**: Convoy Point Visitor Center at the east end of Southwest 328th Street
Hours:	**Glass Bottom Boat Tours**: Daily 10–1. **Snorkeling:** Daily at 1:30. **Scuba diving:** Monday through Friday 9–5, Saturday and Sunday 8:30–1. All trips weather permitting

| Fees: | **Glass Bottom Boat Tours**: Adults $19.95, children under 13 $9.95. Four hour snorkel and scuba diving tour: Adults $27.95 for snorkeling (gear is provided), $34.50 for scuba diving, rental equipment additional, full gear rental $37. Advance reservations required. |
| Phone: | **Park:** (305) 230-1100 |

You only need to smell the air to know you've arrived at the ***Preston B. Bird and Mary Heinlein Fruit and Spice Park***. It is a 20–acre living museum with over 200 species and 500 varieties of fruits, spices, vegetables, herbs, and nuts from around the world. There are more than 100 varieties of citrus alone!

Location:	24801 Southwest 187th Avenue
Hours:	**Park**: Daily 10–5. **Tours:** Saturday and Sunday at 1 and 3 and most afternoons after 12
Fees:	**Park:** Adults $2, children under 12 50¢. **Tours:** Adults $1.50, children under 12 $1
Phone:	(305) 247–5727

Florida City

We've talked about Henry Flagler's railroad as the tours have moved down the east coast. For passengers, Florida City was the last stop before heading to Key West and connecting with a boat train to Havana.

Boy waving to an engineer

Because of its long growing season, Florida has excelled in providing the nation with food. Although citrus crops are best known, the variety of field and tree crops is significant. The ***Florida State Farmer's Market*** lies in the heart of Florida's fruit and vegetable growing country. Although hours vary, stop at the retail stalls to buy some fresh Florida citrus or produce.

Location: 300 North Krome Ave.
Hours: **Market**: Year-round, hours vary.
Phone: (305) 246–6334

Beginning in the 1930s, migrant workers and their families traveled throughout the state bringing in the crops.

Migrant fruit picker, 1937

Key Largo
Islamorada
Indian Key
Big Pine Key
Marathon
Key West

Tour 9.
Hemingway's
Haunts

Expect to be surprised as you drive to the Southernmost tip of the United States along Florida's **Overseas Highway**. It is an engineering marvel that soars from Key to Key across miles of open ocean. The long views of the Gulf of Mexico and the Atlantic Ocean are remarkable, particularly when a summer storm is brewing. The entire trip is so enjoyable that Key West, one of Ernest Hemingway's haunts, becomes an enchanting bonus.

The Florida Keys

The Florida Keys were sighted around 1513 by Ponce de León. Since there is no record that he or any of his crew came ashore, it is thought that he sailed on and landed farther north. By the 1700s and 1800s, the location and isolation of the Keys had been noted by many of the fierce pirates working up and down the Eastern Seaboard. They made the Keys hidden shore havens where they stored their treasures after wrecking ships—or salvaging treasures from ships which had been wrecked during natural storms and hurricanes. By 1822, the buccaneers were so brazen that the U.S. Navy Pirate Fleet was established in Key West. These men had a tough job. Their mission was to control pirates, pillagers, privateers, and professional wreckers—all of whom thrived in the area. Over time, they were successful.

Less than a century later, Henry Flagler extended his Florida East Coast Railroad to Miami. Like many visionaries, he turned to his next challenge. He decided to build a railroad from Miami to Key West and work started in 1905. It took seven years to complete the rail extension that was Henry Flagler's last railroading project. The extension, difficult enough in its own right, was partially wiped out when hurricanes struck the Keys in 1906, 1909, and 1910. These natural catastrophes were ignored.

The era of the railway to Key West ended when a major hurricane struck in 1935. The roadbed was so devastated that no attempt was ever made to repair it. By 1935, automobiles and buses were the tourist's favorite way to travel. Instead of rebuilding the railroad, work began on the *Overseas Highway,* which opened in 1938. It extends for 113 miles and has 43 connecting bridges. For the first time, the entire length of the Florida Keys became easily accessible to residents and travellers.

Key Largo

Lights! Camera! Action!

After Cocoa, this is my favorite town–naming story. Key Largo was originally named Rock Harbor. Then came the movies. Several of the interior shots for *Key Largo* were in Rock Harbor. After the wonderful Humphry Bogart, Lauren Bacall film became famous, residents voted to change the town's name and, in 1952, Key Largo was born. Key Largo is the longest of the Florida Keys.

The first underwater state park in the country is located at the *John Pennekamp Coral Reef State Park*. The park was established to protect and preserve part of the only living coral reef in the continental US. It has 2,350 acres of land and 53,661 acres underwater—extending seven miles into the Atlantic and protects 40 species of coral and 650 species of fish covering approximately 70–nautical square miles of coral reefs, seagrass beds, and mangrove swamps. Enough statistics! This is a perfect spot for scuba divers or those wanting to learn more about the reef. The Visitors Center has a 33,000 gallon aquarium filled with coral formations

and colorful fish. Make plans for a wonderful day on the water, in the water, or under the water. You won't forget the experience.

Location:	Mile Marker 102.5, Overseas Highway, north of Key Largo
Hours:	**Park**: Daily 8–sunset, weather permitting. **Visitor Center**: Daily 8–5. **Glass Botttom Boat Tour**: 9:15, 12:15, 3. **Snorkel Tour:** 9, 12, 3. **Sailing and Snorkeling**: 9, 1:30. Advance reservations recommended, be there one hour before departure for tour.
Fees:	**Park:** $3.25 per vehicle plus 50¢ per person. Persons arriving by foot, bus or bike $1.50. **Glass Bottom Boat Tour**: Adults $15, children under 12 $8.50. **SnorkelingTour**: Adults $23.95, children under 18 $18.95. Rental equipment $4 for mask, fins, and snorkel (you take the snorkel home). **Sailing and Snorkeling**: Adults $28.95, children under 18 $23.95. See above for equipment rental
Phone:	**Park:** (305) 451–1202. **Tours:** (305) 451–1621

As mentioned earlier, pirates thrived throughout the Keys for many years. *Black Caesar's Rock* is a tiny island off the coast. Black Caesar, a Moor, escaped from a slave ship wrecked in the area. He had a business partnership, as it were, with Edward Teach—better known as the pirate Blackbeard. Flying the skull and crossbones, they made a mockery of justice on the seas. The two pirates escaped capture for many years. One of their tricks was to race into Black Rock's harbor, heel over their ship, the *Queen Anne's Revenge,* and attach the masts to a huge iron ring so their potential captors could not see the ship.

During the early 1700s, Black Caesar kept his prisoners and enemies on the island. When he finally moved his pirating operations away from Black Caesar's Rock, the camp was abandoned and the remaining children were left to starve. A few survived and they developed a primitive language. Seminole legends persisted for many years that the area was haunted by savage creatures. Perhaps they were the lost children? In 1718, the *Queen Anne's Revenge* was finally captured and Blackbeard was killed during the battle. Black Caesar tried to blow up the ship, but failed. He was captured, taken to Virginia, and hanged. So ends the story of Black Caesar.

The ***Maritime Museum of the Florida Keys*** shows items recovered from 17th–century sunken wrecks. There is an interesting video that tells the story of the shipwrecks and the treasures that were recovered.

Location:	Mile Marker 102, Overseas Highway
Hours:	Friday through Wednesday 10–5, Sunday 12–5
Fees:	Adults $5, seniors over 55 $4.50, children 6–12 $3
Phone:	(305) 451–6444

Islamorada

Islamorada is a Spanish word meaning Purple Isle, and refers to purple snails found in nearby waters.

One of the most extraordinary experiences to have on the Keys is to swim with the dolphins at the ***Theatre of the Sea***. This is the second oldest marine life park in the world and was created from old quarries used for construction of the Overseas Railroad. In the 1940s, one of the quarries was flooded with sea water and stocked with marine life. We particularly enjoy watching the dolphin show which occurs in a natural coral grotto.

Location:	Mile Marker 84.5, Overseas Highway
Hours:	Daily, 9:30–4
Fees:	**Theatre of the Sea:** Adults $14.75, children 3–12 $8.25. **Special Offerings:** Trainer for a Day $75. Swim with the Dolphins $80. Phone for further information on these special offerings.
Phone:	(305) 664–2431

The Great Hurricane of September 1935 is commemorated here. It had winds of 200 miles an hour. A tidal wave more than 12–feet high was driven inland and swept over the Keys. The barometer dropped to 26.35 inches, the lowest sea level reading in the history of the U.S. Weather Bureau. Entire towns were carried out to sea and more than 800 people died. Sad to say, too few warning signals were given—and most of them were too late.

The Hurricane Memorial reminds us of this tragedy. It includes a raised crypt which holds the remains of a few of the

World War I veterans who lost their lives. The veterans had been part of the Bonus Army. They had not received money for their unpaid bonus certificates and went to Washington in 1934 demanding payment. Instead, they were offered wages of $30–a–month to work on the Overseas Highway. Hundreds of men were out of work. They needed money, left their families and homes, and went to work. It is ironic that the hurricane struck on Labor Day. At the base is a bronze plaque inscribed with an account of the storm and the toll of lives it took.

The Hurricane Memorial

Location:	Mile Marker 79.9, Overseas Highway
Hours:	Daily
Fees:	No charge

Indian Key

In the late 1700s, European commercial ships began using the Gulf Stream and the Bahama Channel. These ocean highways were perilously close to uncharted coral reefs. Ships were often disabled or demolished by reefs, storms, and hurricanes. The area became known when wrecking and salvage crews found their way there to take advantage of treasures they thought they would find. If you have access to a boat, it is possible to tour **Indian Key State Historic Site** and, when you do, think about the following story.

In 1831, Jacob Housman bought the 11 acre island that is now called Indian Key. It became headquarters for his wrecking business which quickly prospered. At one point, there was a permanent settlement of over 60 people, a bowling alley, a hotel, a post office, wharves, and warehouses. However, Jacob Housman was greedy, disreputable, and cruel. In early 1840, he was trying to negotiate a contract with the U.S. Government which would permit him to hunt and kill Indians for $200–a–head. On August 7, 1840, every building in the town, except one, was burned to the ground. It is believed that Chief Chekika and his Indian warriors enacted swift justice. The one building spared was the Post Office where a Masonic apron with its mystic symbols was found spread across a table. Although Jacob Housman and his family survived the fire, he never reestablished his empire and died in a mysterious ship accident six months later.

Today, the *Indian Key State Historic Site* is wonderful for exploring. Spend a few minutes looking out at the horizon imagining Seminoles in dugout canoes, pirate schooners, brigantines, and wreckers all passing along the coast. The tour provides a wonderful history of Indian Key and the Upper Keys.

Location:	Mile Marker 78.5, one mile west of the Overseas Highway and offshore. There is a boat shuttle to Indian Key which departs from Mile Marker 77.5 on the Bay side at Robbie's Marina.
Hours:	Thursday through Monday. Two hour guided walks are conducted at 9 and 1. **Boat shuttle:** Leaves at 8:30 and 12:30 Thursday through Monday
Fees:	**Site:** $1 per person. **Boat shuttle**: Adults $15, children under 12 $10
Phone:	**Site**: (305) 664–4815. **Boat:** Robbie's Marina (305) 664–9814

The San Pedro was a Dutch–built galleon in the New Spain fleet. It left Havana's harbor as part of a convoy of galleons bound for Spain on Friday, the 13th of July 1773 and sank in these waters. The wreck site was uncovered in the 1960s. Plan to take a scuba–swim along the underwater nature trail at the *San Pedro Underwater Archaeological Preserve*—a perfect place to go if you have access to a boat and snorkeling gear. Please respect the fact that NO metal detectors are allowed in the site.

Location:	Mile Marker 78.5, east of the Overseas Highway (1.3 nautical miles south of Indian Key Island) LORAN coordinates 14082.1, 43320.6
Phone:	(305) 664–4815

Once again, a boat is needed. *Lignumvitae Key State Botanical Site* is located on a 280 acre island off Lower Matecumbe Key. The lignumvitae, a native hardwood tree, was called the "tree of life" by the Indians. It is said that the Calusa Indians used the islet as a burial ground.

In 1919 William Matheson, a financier and chemist bought the island for $1 an acre. The house built for his caretaker was made of Dade County pine and Key Largo limestone, a fossil coral rock found on many of the Florida Keys. Most of the stones used were found when the house site was cleared. The building was raised ten feet off the ground to put it above sea level. When you arrive, you step into an unchanged Florida similar to the Florida Keys early tourists and residents found. Exhibits feature pre–Columbian artifacts and items found on Indian Key.

Location:	Mile Marker 78.5, Overseas Highway. There is a boat shuttle to Lignumvitae Key which departs from Mile Marker 77.5 on the Bay side at Robbie's Marina.
Hours:	**Site and House:** Thursday through Monday 8–5. **Boat shuttle:** Leaves at 10 and 2 Thursday through Monday
Fees:	**Site, House, and Tour:** No charge. **Boat shuttle:** Adults $15, children 10
Phone:	(305) 664–4815

Long Key

Henry Flagler established the Long Key Fishing Club which was destroyed by the 1935 hurricane in what is now the *Long Key State Recreation Area*. An especially good time to visit is in March when tiny white butterflies migrate from South America. We also like to hike the Layton Nature Trail which leads through a shaded hummock to the coastline or go canoeing.

Location:	Mile Marker 67.5, Overseas Highway
Hours:	Daily 8–sunset
Fees:	$3.25 per vehicle and 50 cents per person
Phone:	(305) 664–4815

Marathon

When the **Seven Mile Bridge** portion of the Overseas Highway was being built, one of the workers exclaimed that they were involved in a "marathon" task. The name stuck and the town was named. The bridge is the nation's longest continuous span and its 65 foot crest is the highest point in the Florida Keys.

Children enjoy a stop at the **Museum of Crane Point Hammock** and the **Museum of Natural History of the Florida Keys**. This site combines nature trails, a children's museum, a salt water lagoon, a botanical garden, shipwreck artifacts, and a wilderness sanctuary. We particularly enjoy a walk through the coral reef cave or along the boardwalk through a natural hammock.

Location:	Mile Marker 50, 5550 Overseas Highway
Hours:	Monday through Saturday 9–5, Sunday 12–5
Fees:	Adults $7.50, seniors $6, students over 12 $4
Phone:	(305) 743–9100

Big Pine Key

Bahia Honda State Park may be the best sand beach in the Keys. There is a nature trail that goes through a coastal hammock where rare trees and flowers grow. Snorkeling equipment, wet suits, kayaks, and pontoons are available for rent, or bring your own. It's always a lot of fun to swim in the Atlantic Ocean to the south and in Florida Bay to the north. Head to Sandspur Beach to do this. A note of caution, watch out for man–of–wars in the water if the wind is from the south.

Location:	Mile Marker 37, 36850 Overseas Highway
Hours:	Daily 8–sunset
Fees:	One person in vehicle $2.50, two persons in vehicle $5 and 50¢ for each person thereafter
Phone:	**State Park:** (305) 872–2353. **Equipment Rental:** (305) 872–3210

Drive carefully. You are close to the **National Key Deer Refuge**. Walk along the self–guiding Pinewood Nature Trail and watch for the miniature white tail deer, about the size of a large dog. It is an endangered species and is only found in this part of the Keys. Best sighting times are early in the morning and around dusk.

Key Deer

Location:	**Visitor Center:** Mile Marker 29.5 in the Big Pine Shopping Center, Overseas Highway
Hours:	**Refuge**: Daily sunrise to sunset. **Visitor Center:** Monday through Friday 8–5. Closed holidays
Fees:	No charge
Phone:	(305)872–2239

One of the many wonderful places for snorkeling in the Keys is at the **Looe Key National Marine Sanctuary**, which is 6.7 nautical miles southwest of Big Pine Key. Expect to feel that you're part of an aquarium as you swim with the tropical fish. If you scuba dive, there are several wrecked ships, including the 1744 frigate, **HMS Looe**. Contact local dive shops to make arrangements for tours or diving trips.

Key West

Key West is a location and a state of mind. Imagine being in Havana, Cuba in 1822 sitting in a harborside saloon. This is when and where the U.S. Government purchased Key West. The purchase price? It was $2,000.

Start your tour in Old Town Key West. Think about the drive you've taken and the post–pirate environment of the 1880s when the city grew. Notice the town's architecture—a beautiful

blend of Bahamian, Yankee, and Southern. Most homes were built
or adapted for life in the tropics. One of the earliest industries in the
area was sponge fishing. By 1895 the sponge beds had attracted
over 300 boats and 1,400 Greek immigrants. The next influx of
new settlers came when Cuban immigrants began making cigars
here. Over time, the sponge harvesters went to Tarpon Springs and
the cigar makers largely moved to Ybor City and Tampa.

By 1888, Key West was Florida's largest city and the
richest city per capita in America. However, the Depression and
the 1935 hurricane took their toll and the area rapidly declined. Its
reemergence has been largely due to tourism, its tropical climate,
its natural beauty, and—at least on the surface—its relaxed life
style.

Walking is a wonderful way to explore the **Key West
National Historic District.** It extends over a 190 block area in Old
Town Key West and includes an important concentration of
wooden buildings. Historically, the then–island city maintained
close ties with Cuba and much of the architecture was influenced
by that relationship. If your time is limited, particularly note White
Street between the 1000 and 1400 blocks as well as the 800 block
of Virginia Street.

Sometime during your visit, go to **Mallory Square** where
sunset watching is a tradition. It is also a good place to catch the
Conch Train Tour for a 90 minute fully–narrated tour and introduction to Key West and its colorful history.

Location:	One Whitehead Street
Hours:	Daily 9–4:30
Fees:	Adults $15, children 4–12 $7
Phone:	(305) 294–5161

Ernest Hemingway and his wife bought a Spanish colonial–style house in 1931. He lived here for parts of the next 30
years. In 1933, he wrote to a friend,

*We have a fine house here and a yard with fig tree,
lime tree...I could stay here...near all the time....Have
a good place to come back to.*

Now known as the ***Hemingway House and Museum***, the setting and furnishings reflect how things looked when "Papa" Hemingway wrote some of his most famous books. Be sure to visit his writing retreat next to the pool. It was here that he composed such works as ***A Farewell to Arms, The Snows of Kilimanjaro,*** and ***For Whom the Bell Tolls***. The guided tour provides an interesting view of this prolific American writer, his family, and his friends. A word of warning. Stay away if you don't like cats. Ernest Hemingway loved them and had between 50 and 100. Their descendents, at last count over 40, are still very much at home on the property. And, if you really like cats, count their toes—many have six. After your visit, you might want to pick up a copy of ***To Have and Have Not*** and read his story of rum running between Key West and Cuba. It is a colorful addition to the images you will take home.

Location:	907 Whitehead Street
Hours:	Daily 9–5, tours run continuously throughout the day, last tour at 4:30
Fees:	Adults $6.50, children 6–12 $4
Phone:	(305) 294–1575

In 1832, John James Audubon visited Key West while on an expedition painting the tropical birds in the Keys. During this expedition, he sketched 18 species of waterbirds he had never seen before, and five new bird species. When his ***The Birds of America*** series of books was published, 35 birds found in Florida were included. It may be that he spent some time sketching in the gardens, but he never lived at ***Audubon House and Gardens,*** the first restoration in Key West. The beautiful 19th–century home, built for Captain John H. Geiger, is now a museum. It is a Bahamian–style clapboard home, built by ships carpenters and filled with furnishings taken from cargoes of ships that smashed on the treacherous Florida Reef. The house contains a collection of 47 first edition Audubon original engravings as well as fine 18th– and 19th– century antiques.

Location:	205 Whitehead Street at Greene Street
Hours:	Daily 9:30–5
Fees:	Adults $7.50, seniors $6.50, children 6–12, $3.50
Phone:	(305) 294–2116

Howard England had a mission. Starting in early 1970s, he spent nine years digging with a bucket and shovel. He uncovered the country's largest known collection of Civil War cannons at the *Fort Zachary Taylor State Historical Site.* Built between 1845 and 1867, the fort is in the shape of a trapezoid. It was an important site for Union forces during the Civil War. There is a sandy beach on the site that's a good spot for an afternoon picnic.

Location:	End of Southard Street, Truman Annex
Hours:	**Park:** Daily 8–sunset. **Tours:** 12, 2
Fees:	**Park:** One person in vehicle $2.50, two people in vehicle $5, and 50¢ per person thereafter, pedestrians $1.50. **Tours:** No charge
Phone:	(305) 292–6713

Key West's *Lighthouse Museum* tells the story of Florida's third oldest brick lighthouse, built in 1847. Climb the 88 steps to the observation level. The view of the city is remarkable! Then spend some time touring the museum to appreciate the role the lighthouse has played in the history of the Florida Keys.

Key West Lighthouse

Location:	938 Whitehead Street
Hours:	Daily 9:30–5, last admission at 4 pm, closed Christmas
Fees:	Adults $6, children 7–12 $2
Phone:	(305) 294–0012

Walk to *Curry Mansion* for a look at the most ornate house on Key West. When Milton Curry, son of the island's first self–made millionaire was on his honeymoon, he saw a townhouse in Paris. Once back on Key West, he built its adaptation in 1899.

The home has three stories, 11,000 square feet, and 26 rooms. Self–guided tours are available to enjoy the setting and the furnishings.

Location:	511 Caroline Street
Hours:	Daily 10–5
Fees:	Adults $5, children 12 and under $1
Phone:	(305) 294–5349

The *Wrecker's Museum*, also known as the *Oldest House in Key West,* displays ship models, marine artifacts, and a magnificently furnished 1850s Conch–style doll house. The museum is housed in an 1829 Conch house, once home to a local sea captain and wrecker.

Location:	322 Duval Street
Hours:	Daily 10–4, closed Christmas
Fees:	Adults $4, children 3–12 50¢
Phone:	(305) 294–9502

Many artists and writers make Key West home and their work can be seen in the Author's Room at the *East Martello Museum and Art Gallery.* It is housed in a brick Civil War fortress fronting the Atlantic Ocean. It was never used in a battle. There are interesting artifacts about the Keys as well as two permanent art collections on display. The historical section is particularly interesting with exhibits about the Flagler railroad, the cigar–making industry, and sponge diving. In 1949, a Canadian welder named Stanley Papio moved to Key Largo. He started making sculptures in his yard. His works are outstanding and are part of the collection as are the works of Dali, Picasso, and Mario Sanchez, the Cuban–American artist.

Location:	3501 South Roosevelt Boulevard
Hours:	Daily 9:30–5, closed Christmas
Fees:	Adults $6, children 7–15 $2
Phone:	(305) 296–3913

Key West is located at sea level which created challenges at the *Key West Cemetery*. Like New Orleans, all graves are above ground level because of the water table. Unlike New Orleans, coral rock is just under the surface soil. The unique above–ground tombs date back to the 1840s. Particularly note the Monument to the

Cuban Martyrs. It is located at the corner of Palm and Violet and was dedicated to those who died in Cuba's Ten Years' War (1868–1878) against Spanish rule. There is also a monument to the soldiers killed on the **USS Maine**. The battleship explored in Havana Harbor in February 1898. That event signaled the United States' entry into the Spanish–American War which brought about Cuba's independence from Spain. The Cemetery is located at Margaret and Angela Streets and Passover Lane.

We've purposefully created a route so that you have walked through many parts of Key West. Here's one of our favorite Key West homes. Do you remember seeing it?

Now it's time for a sunset. If you feel like being part of a crowd, **Mallory Square** is the place for you. If you'd rather have a quiet experience watching the sun sizzle into the sea, go to **Southernmost Point** and be as far south as possible and still be in the United States.

Wisteria patterned Tiffany lamps

from the

Charles Hosmer Morse Museum of American Art, Winter Park

Central Florida

For many years, Central Florida was noted for the productivity of its citrus groves. However, small, agricultural towns changed rapidly with the arrival of Walt Disney World only little more than 25 years ago. Three tours document the changes.

Tour 10, *Orlando and the Citrus Rim*, highlights the largest city in Central Florida and its Northern communities.

Many people who first come to Florida to enjoy the *Tourist's Mecca* return again and again. West Orange County has become the country's leading tourist destination, with over 40 million visitors vacationing here each year. Tour 11 combines the world class touring with reminders of the ranching era.

The last tour in this section, *Hill Country Adventures,* leads to a college campus with a major collection of Frank Lloyd Wright buildings, visits the highest spot in peninsular Florida to see the gift Edward Bok gave to the state, and stops at Cypress Gardens, the first major theme park in the area.

Packing House Interior, ca. 1939

Orange City
De Land
Mount Dora   Sanford
Lake Weir   Longwood
Maitland   Eatonville
ORLANDO   Winter Park
Christmas

Tour 10.
Orlando
and the
Citrus
Rim

Orlando

Today, over 40 million people visit the greater Orlando area each year. Not everyone is familiar with the area. We urge you to take an extra few minutes and drive extra carefully!

The town was originally settled in the 1840s by Army volunteers who came to Florida to fight the Seminole Wars and decided to stay. By the 1870s, Orlando was a lawless cattle frontier, not unlike Kissimmee and several other Central Florida areas. Beginning in the 1890s, former plantation owners from Civil War states began arriving enticed by climate, water reserves, and relatively inexpensive land. These new residents bought vast tracts of land for about $1 an acre and planted citrus groves. As they established families and expanded their businesses, they led Orlando's evolution from a rough cattle town to a livable community.

For almost 50 years, Orlando stayed a quiet citrus center. Then, change happened quickly! In a series of secret purchases, the Walt Disney organization bought more than 27,000 acres of land. Disney's impact continues to be felt throughout the metropolitan area. Formerly productive orange groves have been harvested to create housing developments and office complexes. Orlando has become an economically diverse city and attracts major industries in a wide variety of fields.

A brisk walk around *Lake Eola* is a good way to look at the cityscape and its urban architecture. After walking around the lake, we like to climb aboard a swanlike paddle boat for another view of the city. If you have time, take a few moments to sit down and enjoy the Japanese garden.

Location:	Downtown at East Central Boulevard
Hours:	**Park**: Daily 7 am to midnight. **Paddle Boats**: Daily noon to 5:30, with seasonal summer extended hours
Fees:	**Park**: No charge. **Boats**: $5.30 per half–hour
Phone:	**Park**: (407) 246–2827

Three of the area's museums are housed in Loch Haven Park.

The *Orange County Historical Museum* includes exhibits on pioneer life on the cattle frontier and the development of central Florida's citrus industry. One of the museum's most popular exhibits is the 1926 Fire Station #3, the oldest standing fire house in the Southeast. It captures the feeling of how the early bucket brigades fought fires.

Location:	812 East Rollins Avenue
Hours:	Monday through Saturday 9–5, Sunday 12–5
Fees:	Adults $2, seniors over 55 $1.50, children 6–12 $1
Phone:	(407) 897–6350

Orlando Firemen, ca. 1890

The *Orlando Museum of Art,* also located in the Loch Haven complex, includes a growing permanent collection of 19th– and 20th–century American art, including works on paper. Make time to see the African art and the fine collection of pre–Columbian artifacts dating from 1200 BC to roughly 1500 AD. Children especially enjoy Art Encounter, a hands–on art exhibit. When the museum is host to an international traveling exhibition, hours and fees may vary.

Location:	2416 North Mills Avenue
Hours:	Tuesday through Saturday 9–5, Sunday 12–5
Fees:	Adults $4, children 4–11 $2
Phone:	(407) 896–4231

Still growing, the *Orlando Science Center and the John Young Planetarium* features hands–on, changing, natural sciences exhibits especially designed for children. Children particularly enjoy the Kidstown, Nature Works, Body Zone, and ShowBiz Science exhibits. We are particularly impressed with the architecture of the new facility.

Location:	777 East Princeton Street
Hours:	Monday through Thursday 9–5, Friday and Saturday 9–9, Sunday 12–5. **Planetarium** and **Cinedome**: Hours are extensive. Closed Thanksgiving and Christmas
Fees:	**Single Adventure/Museum:** Adults $8, seniors $7, children 3–11 $6.50. **Double Adventure/Museum and either Planetarium or Cinedome:** Adults $12, seniors $11, children 3–11 $9.50. **Triple Adventure/Museum, Planetarium, and Cinedome:** Adults $14, seniors $13, children 3–11 $11.50
Phone:	(407) 896–7151

A turn–of–the–century Florida Victorian house serves as the centerpiece of the *Henry P. Leu Botanical Gardens.* This lovely 50 acre park has exceptional walking trails. The largest camellia collection in eastern North America blooms each winter. The gardens include Florida's largest formal rose garden, as well as azaleas, flowering trees, and orchids. This is the perfect spot for a leisurely stroll. In 1936, Henry Leu, a prosperous businessman and Orlando native, bought the property. He and his wife created the gardens. Guided tours through the Leu family homestead show

how a successful citrus grower's family lived between the 1870s and 1901.

Location:	1920 North Forest Avenue
Hours:	**Gardens:** Daily 9–5, extended summer hours. **Tours of the Museum:** Tuesday through Saturday 10–3, Sunday and Monday 1–3, closed Christmas
Fees:	Adults $3, children 6–16 $1
Phone:	(407) 246–2620

An excellent restoration has been accomplished at *Church Street Station.* This complex provides an entertaining visit to the past with three red brick Victorian buildings filled with restaurants, nightclubs, and shops. The period settings are representative of the Gay '90s, the Roaring '20s, and the Wild West.

Location:	129 West Church Street
Hours:	Monday through Friday 11 am–1 am. Saturday and Sunday 11 am–2 am
Fees:	No charge to browse through the area before 6 pm. After 6 pm, admission is charged. Adults $17.95, children 4–12 $10.95
Phone:	(407) 422–2434

Winter Park

Winter Park is one of Orlando's older, more affluent suburbs. If you enjoy shopping, make time to visit Park Avenue, the area's pleasant shopping street. We also recommend a leisurely walk through the adjacent *Rollins College* campus with its Spanish Mediterranean architecture. Head toward the lake on campus and make time to visit the small and excellent *George D. and Harriet W. Cornell Fine Arts Museum*. We especially enjoy their collection of 19th–century American and European art.

Location:	1000 Holt Avenue, on the Rollins College Campus
Hours:	Tuesday through Friday 10–5, Saturday and Sunday 1–5
Fees:	No charge, donations welcome
Phone:	(407) 646–2526

A favorite museum in Winter Park is the *Charles Hosmer Morse Museum of American Art.* It features over 4,000 works, some of which were saved when Laurelton Hall, Louis Comfort Tiffany's Art Nouveau mansion, burned. Of particular interest are the stained glass windows Mr. Tiffany made for Laurelton Hall. There are also works by Frank Lloyd Wright, Maxfield Parrish, and René Lalique. The museum is a marvellous way to examine examples of American art from the 1850s to 1930s.

Location:	445 Park Avenue North
Hours:	Tuesday through Saturday 9:30–4, Sunday 1–4
Fees:	Adults $3, students $1
Phone:	(407) 645–5311

Eatonville

The small town dates back to 1886. It was one of the first communities incorporated by African Americans in the U.S. Within two years after it was founded, its residents had established the government and a school. Zora Neale Hurston, one of the nation's most prolific Black women writers was born in Eatonville and spent her early years here. The town was the setting for *Their Eyes Were Watching God.*

Zora Neale Hurston

Maitland

Pause and consider the past at the *Holocaust Memorial Resource and Educational Center of Central Florida.* The Memorial Wall of Jerusalem commemorates the six million Jews who died. Exhibits outline key Holocaust events.

Location:	851 North Maitland Avenue
Hours:	Monday through Thursday 9–4, Friday 9–1, first and third Sundays 1–4, closed major national and Jewish holidays
Fees:	No charge, donations welcome
Phone:	(407) 628–0555

Threatened and endangered bird species can be seen at the *Florida Audubon Center for Birds of Prey*. Next door, *Audubon House* is a wonderful spot for selecting books and other materials to carry with you as you learn more about Florida's birds.

Location:	1101 Audubon Way
Hours:	Tuesday through Sunday 10–4, closed Christmas and New Year's Day
Fees:	No charge, suggested donation adults $2, children 6–12 $1
Phone:	(407) 644–0190

Jules Andre Smith founded the *Maitland Art Center* in 1937 and established his Research Studio here. Stucco buildings are highly decorated with murals, bas–reliefs, and carvings done in Aztec–Mayan "Fantasy" architecture. Browse through the museum, walk through the Research Studio's courtyard, and spend a few moments in the chapel.

Location:	231 West Packwood Avenue
Hours:	Monday through Friday 10–4:30, Saturday and Sunday 12–4:30, closed major holidays
Fees:	No charge, donations welcome
Phone:	(407) 539–2181

Sanford

In 1871, General Henry R. Sanford, former U.S. Minister to Belgium, bought 12,000 acres of land. Unable to obtain labor to clear the land and plant citrus groves, he sent an agent to Sweden. The agent recruited 100 workers by offering them passage, all expenses, and a five–acre grove in return for a year's work. Thus began the Swedish settlement in the area.

The *Central Florida Zoological Park* has over 150 species of native and exotic animals, birds, and reptiles. We particularly enjoy seeing the kookaburra exhibit and the botanical garden.

Location:	3755 Highway 17–92, 2 miles west of Sanford
Hours:	Daily, 9–5, closed Thanksgiving and Christmas
Fees:	**Park:** No charge. **Zoo:** Adults $7, seniors over 60 $4, children 3–12 $3. Seniors half price on Tuesdays
Phone:	(407) 323–4450

Orange City

Louis Thursby built one of the first landings along the St. Johns River and developed Blue Springs as a steamboat tourist stop on the waterway. In 1872, the Thursbys built their frame house on top of an ancient shell mound. It was built from three kinds of center–cut pine, milled in Savannah, Georgia and transported by boat to the site. The ***Thursby House*** has been restored to look as it would have in the 1875–1887 period. Note the cypress water holding tank. With so much water around, it was necessary to have a supply of drinkable water.

B*lue Springs State Park* is also a wonderful place for viewing manatees from mid–November to the end of March, depending on the weather. Begin your visit by seeing the interpretive exhibits on Florida's springs and the manatees, also known as "sea cows." They weigh about a ton and are attracted to ***Blue Springs State Park*** because of the warmth of the St. Johns River and the hot spring. Step onto the wooden walkway with its observation platforms built over the run that extends from the spring boil to the river. When the manatees are in the run, it is amazing to see them so close. When they are not in the run, you can swim and scuba dive. This is also a fine spot for a hike.

Location:	2100 West French Avenue
Hours:	Daily 8 to sunset
Fees:	**Park**: $4 per vehicle with up to eight people, $2 for one person in a car, $1 for walk ins or bikers. **Scuba Diving:** Bring your own equipment. Fee is $5.30 per diver and each diver must have a partner. Register between 8 and 3.
Phone:	(904) 775–3663

Mount Dora

Sailing, antiquing, and sightseeing are among the charms of this 19th century town. Go exploring and find the **Donnelly House,** built in 1893 by one of the town's first promoters and its first mayor. It is one of the best examples of Steamboat Gothic architecture remaining in Florida.

Zellwood

Bob White Field is a perfect place to see vintage planes. At 3,300–feet in length, this is one of the longest grass airstrips in Florida and is home to about 40 vintage planes. Pack a picnic and some folding chairs and visit on a weekend to watch these beautiful planes in action.

Location:	7011 West Jones Avenue, one mile west of Highway 441
Hours:	Daily 9–6
Fees:	No charge
Phone:	(407) 886–3180

DeLand

Henry A. DeLand, baking powder manufacturer, founded the community in 1876. In 1889, Lue Gim Gong moved here. His mother had taught him ancient Chinese horticultural methods which he used to perfect and introduce a new variety of orange. By 1892, he had perfected the Gim Gong grapefruit which withstood 10 degrees greater cold than other varieties developed to that time. His contributions were immeasurable to the emerging citrus field.

Stetson University is a good destination for a walk. The **Gillespie Museum of Minerals** houses the second largest private collection of minerals in the world. Be sure to see the 130 pound topaz and take the self–guided tour.

Location:	234 East Michigan Avenue, Stetson University
Hours:	Monday through Friday 9–12, 1–4, closed holidays
Fees:	No charge, donations welcome
Phone:	(904) 822–7330

Christmas

Take Highway 50 east from Orlando to the **Christmas Post Office.** This tiny working post office is where to come if you want your cards to have an "authentic" Christmas postmark and a green Christmas tree design. The rubber hand stamp was designed by the 1930s postmaster in the 1930s. Today's postmistress recommends getting cards to the post office by early December to be sure they have time to hand stamp them.

If you're ready for a good hike, visit the **Tosohatchee State Reserve** which has foot paths, bike ways, and horse trails. By the way, the park is named after the Tootoosahatchee Creek—probably shortened to pronounce and fit on the sign! This is a beautiful wilderness area. No facilities are provided.

Location:	Taylor Creek Road, off Route 50 in Christmas
Hours:	Daily 8–sundown
Fees:	**Reserve:** $2 per car. **Overnight Backpack Camping** (no RVs): Adults $3, children $2
Phone:	(407) 568–5893

Tour the reconstructed 1837 **Fort Christmas Historical Park and Museum.** The fort was built between December 25–27, 1837—hence the name. What you see is a replica of the type of bulwark used for protection against Indians during the Second Seminole War. The Visitor Center is housed in a replica of an old cracker home. Tours are given telling about the pioneer life of early Florida settlers, 1910–1920. Please phone ahead for tour reservations.

Location:	1300 Fort Christmas Road, Route 420
Hours:	Tuesday through Saturday 10–5, Sunday 1–5
Fees:	No charge
Phone:	(407) 568–4149

Alligators, with a bite...

Have a fascinating day learning about them

at Gatorland Zoo.

Alligators are found where
you least expect them—on golf courses,
in lakes, sometimes in back yards.
If it looks like a log and moves, watch out!
Keep yourself, your children, and
your animals away from them
and never, ever even think of feeding them.

Tour 11.
The
Tourist's
Mecca

Sometime during their stay, many Floridians and most tourists head to the Tourist's Mecca. The area is unlike anything else in Florida. There are world–class attractions, amusements, hotels, restaurants, and recreational facilities. Let's go!

Lake Buena Vista

Only a little more than 25 years ago, Lake Buena Vista was a tiny crossroad town in the middle of woodlands, wetlands, and orange groves. It is now the host community for *Walt Disney World*. There is so much to do that —given the time, the stamina, and the resources—one could easily spend a week or two without leaving Disney property.

Location:	Disney complex off I–4 West of Orlando
Hours:	Daily 9–6 (or later). Hours vary by park and season.
Fees:	Adults $42.14, children 3–9 $33.92, ask about multiple day guest passes
Phone:	(407) W–DISNEY for reservations and information

Within this section, the approach is not to guide you through every activity. Rather, it is to highlight some of my favorite things to see and do. When you arrive on Disney property, ask for a map and an outline of the hours, shows, and special activities at each park. Don't hesitate to ask questions. There are well marked and well staffed guest service areas at each park, at each Disney hotel on property, and at Disney Village Marketplace. Take a few minutes to consider what you want to do and then prepare for fun, adventure, and surprises. One last bit of advice, wear comfortable shoes and take frequent rest and water breaks. There's a lot of ground to cover!

Four recommendations are offered to help maximize your enjoyment of the parks. First, if you arrive as the doors open, head for the farthest point from the entrance and work your way back. You'll miss some crowds this way. Second, accept lines as part of the overall experience. Use your in line time for people watching, tee shirt reading, solving the world's problems, or whatever. Lines move quickly and are often shorter than posted wait times. Third, take a break in the early afternoon for a swim or a nap. Consider the break as a reenergizing stop. The pause is particularly important if you are traveling with children. Fourth, plan to return to the parks in the late afternoon and stay through the evening.

See as many of the evening events as possible—they are marvelous! Our order of preference? The fireworks and laser show at EPCOT, the parade at the Magic Kingdom, and the fireworks show at the Disney–MGM Studios.

Disney-MGM Studios

First stop is the ***Disney–MGM Studios Theme Park.*** It combines tours, rides, and adventures with working movie and TV studios—and larger–than–life–size outdoor sets. If your time here is limited, the following are six of our all–time favorite things to do.

Tower of Terror 2 gives you a chance to plunge 13 stories. Practice screaming before starting this experience! The Great Movie Ride provides an animated review of the development of movies in America. It brings back memories of old classics, legendary stars, and recent thrillers! Robin Williams and Walter Cronkite serve as the improbable hosts for the extraordinary Animation Tour which shares the development of animation and gives you the chance to watch Disney animators at work on current projects. The Backstage Tour leads you behind the scenes at the working studio. Star Tours combines flight simulator technology with laser graphics and a chance to do a little of your own space traveling. If you think you understand the limitations of 4–D, see the Muppets 3–D Show twice. Its innovations are outstanding!

By now there's a good chance that you're getting ready for a rest. Consider a Hollywood–style meal at the Brown Derby— perhaps the original Cobb Salad and a slice of grapefruit cake.

EPCOT

Consider taking the launch from the Studios to the International Gateway entrance to **EPCOT.** The route allows you to enjoy some amazing hotel architecture and lets you enter at the World Showcase. Make time to see films, look at exhibits, meet the Norwegian troll in an action–packed ride, and go shopping at the Chinese and Japanese Pavilions. However, World Showcase is only part of the EPCOT experience.

After circling the World, slowly head toward the "golf ball." On your way, make time for several hours of imaginative entertainment. We particularly enjoy the Energy Pavilion and the hands–on activities near the entrance. Be among the first to try Test Track. It is Disney's fastest (65 m.p.h.) and largest (150,000 square feet) ride. Learn how test engineers design safer cars and then climb into a test vehicle at the General Motors proving ground. Hold on!

Our favorite restaurant stop for dinner is the outdoor cafe at the French Pavilion for a moderately priced French meal. If you're tired, the cafe provide a good view of the laser and fireworks show while dining and sipping iced tea or a glass of French wine.

The Magic Kingdom

The **Magic Kingdom** is made up of seven lands. Of all the Disney theme parks, this is a fine first stop for children. They meet some of their favorite Disney characters in an area on Main Street. Teenagers naturally gravitate to Space Mountain and the Big Thunder Mountain Railroad. Don't miss the Haunted Mansion, Pirates of the Caribbean, and the Jungle Cruise. Mickey's Toontown Fair is special for little ones. In the evening, Spectro–Magic uses fibre optics and ministrobes to light the floats, creating visual surprises throughout the parade!

First time visitors often limit their Disney adventure to the theme parks, but there is so much more to see and do.

The Nature Preserve

Rarely crowded, **Discovery Island** is an 11 acre island haven for birds, mammals, reptiles, and people. Take a launch from the **Contemporary Resort** or **Fort Wilderness** and spend a relaxing few hours following the nature trail.

Location:	Disney complex off I–4 West of Orlando
Hours:	Daily 10–5:30
Fees:	Adults $12.67, children 3–9 $6.89
Phone:	(407) W–DISNEY

The Water Parks

If the day is hot and you're ready for another kind of Disney experience, try **Typhoon Lagoon, Blizzard Beach** or **River Country.** Each of these family–oriented water theme parks has frightening white water raft rides for teenagers, a little kids' area with pint–sized water games. At **Typhoon Lagoon** there is a drifting, lazy river inner–tube float for all ages. Beach chairs, sand, and the giant wave maker provide a good alternative for hot weather enjoyment. **Blizzard Beach** transports you right to winter, with a Florida twist. **River Country** is more rustic. Leave the crowds behind at Fort Wilderness and find the nature walk to the Ol' Swimming Hole.

Location:	Disney Complex off I–4 West of Orlando
Hours:	Daily 10–5
Fees:	**Blizzard Beach and Typhoon Lagoon:** Adults $26.45, children 3–9 $20.67. **River Country:** $16.95, children 3–9 $13.25
Phone:	(407) W–DISNEY

Disney Institute

A wonderful change for the visitor interested in combining a world–class vacation with the opportunity to learn animation, try gourmet cooking, go rock climbing, perfect a golf game, or do more than 50 other recreational and learning activities. Guests stay at the Institute in comfortable bungalows. Most evenings nationally known musicians or film makers share their skills and ideas with Institute guests. Oh, yes, there's also a wonderful spa and special activities for children. Need I say more? This is a Disney experience that helps you create your vacation at your own pace.

Location:	Disney complex West of Orlando
Phone:	(407) W–DISNEY

Shopping, Evening Entertainment, and More

Downtown Disney is the expanded Disney Village Marketplace and Pleasure Island area. It combines shopping, dining, children's activities, and evening entertainment. Although there are many places to shop, our first stop is always the *World of Disney Store.* You won't believe how many items carry the Mickey logo until you spend an hour or so browsing in this Disney megastore. Pause for a matinee to a midnight movie at the 24-screen movie theater. Hopefully you'll get hungry during your visit. The themed restaurants and clubs are a fun way to combine a meal and an entertainment experience. Joining Planet Hollywood and the Rainforest Cafe are Gloria Estefan's Bongos Cuban Cafe, the Wolfgang Puck Cafe, and a House of Blues.

Pleasure Island is perfect for night owls and those with lots of energy. Comedy Warehouse, the Adventurer's Club, and the Neon Armadillo, a country and western club, are all there. There is also dancing, indoors and out, an outdoor bandstand and—as if all that isn't enough—every night is New Year's Eve with a countdown, fireworks, confetti, and the works! Bring your dancing shoes. There are now seven venues, including a Jazz Club.

Location:	Disney complex West of Orlando
Hours:	Daily 7 pm to 2 am
Fees:	After 7 pm, $19.03 for all. Valid ID required for persons over 18, parent or guardian must accom–pany anyone under 18
Phone:	(407) W–DISNEY

Office Architecture

Disney continues to make major architectural statements and, over the past several years, has been particularly committed to post–Modernism. Watch for the office buildings between Disney Village and Pleasure Island. *Team Disney*, designed by Arata Isozaki, is partially Bauhaus, partially Cubist, and uniquely Disney. It houses the world's largest sundial. The *Casting Center* is imaginative in a more whimsical way. Particularly notice the details outside the building and along the corridor leading to the reception center.

Hotel Architecture

Disney hotels are part of the wraparound destination resort experience. Properties range from luxurious to whimsical. The always elegant *Grand Floridian* is particularly beautiful during the holiday season. A special afternoon pause is High Tea served just beyond the main lobby. The *Yacht and Beach Clubs* provide a setting of subdued, beachside elegance and are located just a few minutes away from EPCOT. Designed by Robert A. M. Stern, pay particular attention to the finishing details used throughout the buildings. Nearby are two hotels designed by Michael Graves, the *Swan* and the *Dolphin*. The exteriors and interiors are unexpected and particularly interesting to see when accompanied by children. Listen for and enjoy their reactions as they discover the many features. Disney's newest addition is the *Boardwalk*, reminiscent of seaside resorts on the Eastern Seaboard.

... and Next

Scheduled to open in 1998, plan to visit *Disney's Animal Kingdom* which will combine live and make–believe animals, including animatronic dinosaurs. Also, watch for *Cirque du Soleil*.

Also in the Lake Buena Vista Area

The *Hyatt Regency Grand Cypress* is a world–class hotel. Located near the Disney property, it combines convenience to the theme parks with quiet elegance. Sunday is a good time to visit and enjoy brunch. After dining, you'll probably want to take a walk. Although there is a fitness trail, a leisurely stroll around the pool and through the gardens is recommended to see the impressive Asian, European, and American art and sculpture.

Location:	60 Grand Cypress Boulevard
Phone:	(407) 239–1234

Kissimmee

The Calusa Indian name for what is now Kissimmee was Heaven's Place. Although white settlement to the area began in 1878, it was the arrival of Hamilton Disston, a Philadelphia millionaire, which would change the area's future. On the surface, it was simple enough. In 1880, Hamilton. Disston came to Florida to fish on East Tohopekaliga Lake. William Bloxham, Florida's Governor at the time, invited himself along on the fishing outing. The Governor knew Mr. Disston was interested in Florida real estate and Florida was broke. They fished, they talked, and they struck a deal.

A year later, the State of Florida sold Hamilton Disston and his partners four million acres of land for 25¢ an acre. The land extended from north of Tarpon Springs on the west coast to more than halfway across Central Florida, and as far south as Lake Okeechobee. Think of its value today!

The land purchase served three important purposes for the State of Florida. It replenished a flat treasury, it attracted monied investors' attention to Florida's real estate, and it emphasized the state's interest in developing its land. The precedent for land deals in return for development opened the way for other entrepreneurs, including the railroaders who would arrive shortly.

Hamilton Disston and his associates cleared and drained land, created canals, and began the development process. Unfortunately, he died before realizing the great financial benefits his farsighted negotiations and investment caused to happen.

It is interesting to note that seven years after Mr. Disston arrived, a young family bought an orange grove near Kissimmee. Their names were Flora and Elias Disney. A few years later they moved to Chicago where their son, Walter Elias, was born. We can only wonder if his family's early knowledge of central Florida had an impact on Walt Disney's major purchase in the area little more than half a century later.

Originally known as Cow Town, Kissimmee has a colorful history. In 1895, Frederic Remington arrived to sketch, sculpt, and draw the cattlemen. He was not impressed. In sharp lines, he etched the portrait of a Cracker cowboy. As he later told his story, Kissimmee was a frontier town that was so wild that even seasoned ranchers stayed safely inside at night.

Today, the community serves two publics. On one hand, it continues to serve as a regional trading center for the area's ranching operations. It also is one of the largest tourist support areas in the country with many hotels, attractions, and restaurants.

The *Flying Tigers Warbird Air Museum* is dedicated to restoring World War II aircraft to flying condition. Since many of the planes are privately owned, the collection on display is constantly changing. Retired servicemen who know and love airplanes and aviation history serve as guides for an interesting 45–minute tour. Biplane tours are available with advance reservations.

Location:	231 North Hoagland Boulevard
Hours:	Monday through Saturday 9–6, Sunday 9–6. Closed Christmas
Fees:	**Museum:** Adults $6, seniors over 60 and children under 12 $5. **Biplane Tours:** $95 to $180
Phone:	(407) 933–1942

One of the largest alligator attractions in Florida is *Gatorland Zoo*. With over 50 acres, it combines a working alligator farm, a zoo, allegator shows, and a narrow gauge railroad tour. Enter the sprawling park through the jaws of a giant gator. Walk along a boardwalk through an allegator infested marsh. Stop at a sandpit surrounded to watch a Gator Wrestling match. Don't miss the daily Gator Jumparoos where allegators compete for dead chickens hanging from ropes. It's effective in reminding us to stay far, far away from those fast moving critters. The Snakes of Florida exhibit is interesting. We also enjoy walking along the boardwalk through the beauty of the cypress swamp. We urge you to make time for this outstanding facility. It feels a long distance, in time and space, from most of the rest of what you'll see in this part of central Florida.

Location: 14501 South Orange Blossom Trail
Hours: Daily 9–sunset
Fees: Adults $13.95, seniors over 55 $11.83, children
                 10-12 $8.95, children 3-9 $6.48. One child 3-9 free
                 with each paying adult guest
Phone: (407) 855–5496 or 800–393–JAWS

Unincorporated Orange County
Lights, Camera, Action, and Splash

Return to the Tourist's Mecca with a trip along International Drive and Kirkman Road.

Sea World of Florida has several new exhibits. Be sure to see Terrors of the Deep, featuring fearsome underwater creatures. The exhibit has multiple aquariums and the visitor feels immersed in the underseas world of eels, sharks, barracudas, sea snakes, and other predators from the deep. Another of our favorite activities is the Whale and Dolphin Discovery Show.

Location: 7007 Sea World Drive
Hours: Daily 9–10, closing times may vary by season
Fees: Adults $40.95, children 3–9 $33.95
Phone: (407) 351–3600

Universal Studios Florida is a combination theme park and working sound stages and sets for TV and movie production. It is growing quickly and is in the midst of a $2 billion dollar expansion which will quadruple its size and attractions. More about them in a few minutes.

A few of our favorite rides include the following. Terminator II, is a superb and exciting total 3-D sensory experience. You won't forget it! The Back to the Future Ride is exceptional. It is bumpy, adventuresome, imaginative, technically sophisticated, and not recommended for people with weak stomachs. If you take the ride, you will probably want to go again to try to figure out how all of those wonderful special effects happened. Also be sure to experience Earthquake and Psycho. Other favorite attractions are the Wild West Stunt Show and the Animal Show. This location demands a full day, or two, or more. Go early, take a break in the afternoon, and return for more touring, a slow walk through the lifelike sets, and the evening stunt show on the lagoon.

Looking ahead at *Universal Studios*, watch for *CityWalk Orlando* due to open in fall of 1998 which will add dozens of nightclubs, restaurants, and theaters for evening activities. Islands of Adventure will open soon. It includes dueling roller coasters, with opposing cars coming within a foot of each other. Spider–Man will combine live action, 3–D, and a simulator as you feel like you're taking a 400–foot drop. We're especially eager to see Stephen Spielburg's Jurassic Park area, much larger than the wonderful Jurassic attraction that is already open. There will also be four other islands including the Lost Continent, Seuss Landing, Toon Lagoon, and Marvel Universe, all of which open during the summer of 1999. So, come for a visit now and plan a repeat trip in a few years to catch these new attractions.

Location:	1000 Universal Studios Plaza
Hours:	Daily 9-7. Closing times vary by season
Fees:	Adults $42.14, children 3–9 $33.92; ask about multiple day passes
Phone:	(407) 363–8000

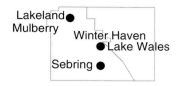

Tour 12.
Hill
Country
Adventures

Fasten your seat belt! Tour 12 travels along the highest land in peninsular Florida. This would be a major statement in most states. In peninsular Florida the highest point of land is just over 300 feet above sea level. So, no oxygen masks are needed.

Lakeland

Lakeland's contemporary history began with the coming of the South Florida Railroad in 1884. Henry Plant worked to establish a railway system on the West Coast during the same period that Henry Flagler was building his railway on the East Coast. Lakeland serves as a trading center for the agricultural and mining communities nearby.

Architect Frank Lloyd Wright came to Florida in 1938 at the request of an administrator at *Florida Southern College*. For over 20 years, he created the Child of the Sun Collection of buildings. Twelve structures create the largest one-site concentration of Frank Lloyd Wright's work in the world. If you visit when school is in session, go to the Administration Building for a self-guided tour brochure and and to see examples of Mr. Wright's designs in decorative arts and furnishings. Another good time to visit is on Sunday morning to see the *Annie Pfeiffer Chapel*, one of the buildings he designed. Go to the second level, look through the windows, and enjoy an overview of the entire collection.

Location:	North Shore of Lake Hollingsworth.
Hours:	Daily
Fees:	No charge
Phone:	(941) 680-4131

Young people particularly enjoy seeing the flight simulator and hands-on aircraft at the *Sun 'n Fun Air Museum* where you can also see a large collection of experimental aircraft, For adults, the experimental aircraft and the hands-on workshop are fascinating.

Location:	4175 Medulla Road
Hours:	Monday through Friday 9-5, Saturday 10-4, Sunday 12-4
Fees:	Adults $4, children $2
Phone:	(941) 644-0741

Mulberry

At least ten million years ago, the ocean flooded the area now called Florida. As the waters washed through the state, billions of phosphate particles were deposited on the land. These particles, along with sand and clay, settled into strata. The retreating waters eventually buried the phosphate beds under tons of sandy soil, mostly in central Florida. This area became known as Bone Valley because of the bones and fossilized remains of prehistoric animals common to phosphate deposits. The City of Mulberry, in the heart of this district, has long been known as the phosphate capital of the world.

The town itself was named for a large mulberry tree that grew near the railroad tracks. In the old days, shipments were simply marked, "Put off at the big mulberry tree." Riding through town today, it is difficult to realize that less than a century ago Mulberry was filled with gamblers and outlaws all drawn to the area because of the phosphate mines. Mulberry looked like a Western gold mining town where saloons, dance halls, and chaos were often the only order of the day.

Visit the **Mulberry Phosphate Museum** which contains bones and fossil artifacts from Florida's prehistoric era. One of the finds is a Baleen whale skeleton, which is over 10 million years old and more than 18 feet long. Children always enjoy searching for fossils in the rock pile.

Location:	State Road 37 South, just behind City Hall
Hours:	Tuesday through Saturday 10-4:30
Fees:	No charge, donations welcome
Phone:	(941) 425-2823

Sebring

George Sebring was a pottery manufacturer from Sebring, Ohio. He planned his town based on the pattern of Heliopolis, the mythological City of the Sun. Streets radiate from a central park which represents the sun.

Children's Museum of the Highlands features hands-on interpretive exhibits for children of all ages. This is a "please touch" facility. Children are encouraged to explore and experiment on their own. Exhibits include the Speed of Sound exhibit which gives kids a chance to "see" the speed of their own voice. The House of Design begins with circles and squares. Going to an architect's table, youngsters find out what it takes to design a building. At the Bubble Image see how you would look inside a huge bubble—or blow smaller bubbles and watch them float through the museum. This is a fun location for youngsters!

Location:	219 North Ridgewood Drive
Hours:	Tuesday through Saturday 10-5, Thursday 10-8
Fees:	General admission $2, children must be accompanied by an adult
Phone:	(941) 385-5437

Explore the natural world at *Highland Hammock State Park* by stopping for the interpretive booklet and taking a hike along one of the nature trails. There is an interesting *Civilian Conservation Corps Museum* housed in a 1930s building constructed of native lumber, and built on site by Conservation Corps workers. A paved drive winds through the hammock and there are several short hiking trails off the road. Watch for sunning alligators and orchids.

Location:	5931 Hammock Road
Hours:	**Park:** Daily 8-sunset. **Museum:** Open daily, hours vary by the season. **Nature Tram Tour:** Tuesday through Friday at 1, Saturday and Sunday at 1 and 2:30. **Walks:** November through April on Thursday evenings, hours vary. **Slide Presentation:** Saturday evenings, hours vary. Call ahead for time information.
Fees:	**Park:** $3.25 per vehicle for up to 8 people per vehicle, walk-ins and bikers $1. **Museum:** No charge
Phone:	(941) 386-6094

Lake Wales

Lake Wales is named for the geographer who first determined that this area was at the geographic center of the state. In its early days, sales of timber and turpentine supported the residents.

Bok Tower Gardens brings joy to the spirit. Edward Bok was a Norwegian immigrant who became publisher of the *Ladies Home Journal*. In 1923, he bought the ridge land at the top of Iron Mountain at the exact center of the state. It had once been the sacred ground where Seminole

Bok Tower

Indians came to worship. Mr. Bok selected Frederick Law Olmsted, Jr. to convert the scrub and orange grove into his beautiful sanctuary. When the facility was completed in 1929, Mr. and Mrs. Bok gave the property to the American people. Mr. Bok felt it should be a palace of renewal, a haven where world weary visitors might stop and rest and gaze from the 295 foot elevation and listen to the music of the carillon.

Before walking through part of the 130 acre gardens to the tower, watch the narrated slide presentation in the newly designed, Mediterranean Revival-style Visitor Center complex. Then walk up the hill to the Overlook which is located at the highest point on the property. The valley you see below was part of the ocean floor half a million years ago. *Bok Tower* is the centerpiece of the facility. It was constructed of pink and gray Georgia marble and Florida coquina stone. Sculpture covers parts of the tower with Florida's herons, pelicans, flamingos, geese, and swans. The 205 foot tall singing tower is considered one of the world's great carillons. The Tower houses a 57 bell carillon. It was cast in Loughborough, England. The largest bell, the Bourdon, weighs over 11 tons—the smallest treble weighs 17 pounds. Although not open to the public, the Tower's brass Creation Door, with its 30 panels, is impressive. If you could enter, you would find the largest carillon library in the world on one of the upper floors. A 45 minute concert occurs each day at 3 pm. The bronze bells fill the air with sacred works, or ragtime, or classical music. In addition, melodies also fill the air every half hour beginning at 10 am. This is a very special oasis.

Location:	1151 Tower Boulevard, 3 miles North of Lake Wales off Highway 27
Hours:	**Gardens:** Daily 8-5. **Visitor Center:** Daily 9-5. **Guided Nature Walks:** January 15-April 15: Daily 12 and 2
Fees:	Adults $4, children 5-12 $1
Phone:	(941) 676-1408

We talked about Kissimmee's wild frontier earlier. You can recapture a bit of that scene today with a visit to the *Lake Kissimmee State Park.* The 5,030 acre park has 13 miles of hiking trails to explore. Climb the observation tower which provides a magnificent view of Lake Kissimmee.

Within the park the *Kissimmee Cow Camp* provides a living-history interpretation of the area's cattle country, circa 1876. The stories of the Florida cowboys are wonderful and you can easily spend an afternoon watching the kids imagine the good old days. Talk with a "cow hunter." His job was to round up strays and drive them to boats for the journey to market in Cuba. The Park Ranger describes life during the post-Civil War era.

Location:	14248 Camp Mack Road, off Boy Scout Road which is off Route 60
Hours:	**Park:** Daily 7 to sunset. **Cow Camp:** Saturday, Sunday, and major holidays 9:30-4:30
Fees:	$3.25 per car, including up to 8 people per vehicle, walk-ins and bikers $1
Phone:	(941) 696-1112

Winter Haven

Winter Haven is located exactly midway between the Gulf of Mexico and the Atlantic Ocean, 75 miles from each shore.

The granddaddy of all of Florida's outdoor theme parks is *Cypress Gardens.* In the 1930s, Dick Pope, a master tourism promoter for Central Florida, and his family developed the 233 acre center. His aim was to make it a facility where families would have fun together. It is said that Walt Disney took his children there and spent time in the parking lot noticing the large number of out–of–state license plates and the larger number of families visiting.

Walkways lead through acres of beautiful, towering cypress trees that provide shade for over 7,000 varieties of flowers and plants from over 75 countries. If you do nothing else, make time for the Botanical Gardens and the water ski show. We also particularly enjoy Wings of Wonder, a glass-enclosed, Victorian-style conservatory containing more than 1,000 free-flying butterflies. In addition, there is an Animal Forest Zoological Park.

Location:	2641 South Lake Summit Drive, State Road 540, East of Winter Haven
Hours:	Daily 9:30-5:30, seasonal hours vary
Fees:	Adults $29.50, seniors over 55 $24.50, children 6-9 $19.50
Phone:	(941) 324-2111

Mr. Pope did a great deal to promote water activities and water skiing. He attracted Esther Williams to *Cypress Gardens*, built a swimming pool for her use, and probably helped oversee her films that were produced here. Plan to tour the *Water Ski Museum and Hall of Fame* which traces the sport from 1922. This is the place to see the first water ski ever built and learn its story. Now what about the boats? Come here to see a fine collection of classic boats and motors.

Location:	799 Overlook Drive Southeast
Hours:	Monday through Friday 10-5, closed major holidays
Fees:	No charge, donations welcome
Phone:	(941) 324-2472

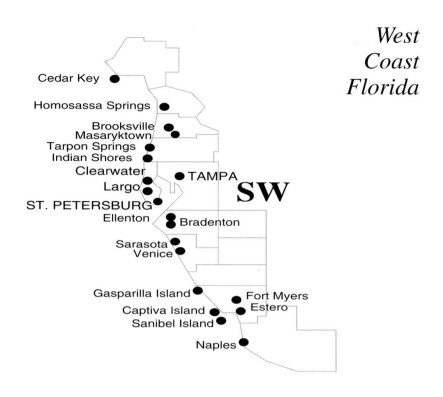

The communities curving around the West Coast of the Gulf of Mexico are quite different from those you visited along the state's East Coast.

Tampa and St. Petersburg are two major cities in this area. They have a friendly rivalry, cater to different audiences, and serve as a *Dynamic Duo* for business and industry as is described in Tour 13.

The Greatest Show on Earth winters on the West Coast. Take Tour 14 and learn about the Ringlings, Sarasota, and two of America's greatest inventors.

An entirely different mood prevails along the Northern portion of the West Coast. Time slows down as you drive toward Cedar Key. Enjoy a leisurely drive through hardwood forests as you find the *Time–Lapse Territory* described in Tour 15.

Tampa Bay Hotel, ca. 1891,

and a

view from the front porch a few years later.

Tour 13.
The Dynamic Duo
Tampa and St. Petersburg

Tampa and St. Petersburg maintain a friendly rivalry. St. Pete combines a beach community with an active business community. Over the past several decades, Tampa has grown rapidly and has emerged as a modern, metropolitan city.

Tampa

In 1884, Henry B. Plant extended his railroad and shipping system to Tampa. When he arrived, the city was a small town with 700 residents. Because of his remarkable economic efforts, the population expanded to 5,000 residents during the next six years and, in 1891, he opened the opulent *Tampa Bay Hotel* as a fashionable railroad resort. It was the first large, fully electrified building in Tampa and was promoted as the world's most elegant hotel. The building is a treasure with ornate Moorish architecture, domed towers, and bulbous minarets topped with silver crescents. The building is considered the finest example of Moorish architecture in the Western Hemisphere.

During the Spanish–American War, about 30,000 troops camped in the Tampa area. Then Colonel Teddy Roosevelt trained his Rough Riders on the hotel grounds and the hotel served as headquarters for American troops. Frederic Remington might have been working on his charcoal sketches. Winston Churchill, a young reporter in 1898, stayed at the hotel while covering the War. Clara Barton, founder of the Red Cross, had her headquarters in the city and was preparing to help the injured.

Today, the hotel building houses the *Henry B. Plant Museum* as well as part of the *University of Tampa.* The museum recreates the opulent life–style of railroad entrepreneur Henry B. Plant, his hotel, and tourism in the early days. Make time to walk through the Spanish–American War Room.

Location:	401 West Kennedy Boulevard
Hours:	**Museum**: Tuesday through Saturday 10–4, Sunday 12–4, **Campus tour**: September through May, Tuesday and Thursday at 1:30. Museum closed and no tours on Thanksgiving, Christmas and New Year's Day. Phone ahead for reservations
Fees:	**Museum**: Donations welcome, suggested amount adults $3, children under 13 $1 **Campus tour**: no charge
Phone:	(813) 254–1891

Tampa's *Museum of Art* has a large permanent collection including Greek and Roman antiquities as well as 19th–and 20th–century paintings. Be sure to see the photography exhibits and the sculpture collection.

Location:	600 North Ashley Drive
Hours:	Monday through Saturday 10–5, Wednesday open until 9 pm, Sunday 1–5. **Tours:** Call for schedule
Fees:	Adults $5, seniors over 62 and students with ID $4, children 6–18 $3
Phone:	(813) 274–8130

The *Museum of African–American Art* contains paintings and sculpture focusing on a people and a nation. Included are works by Edward Bannister, Romare Bearden, and Henry Tanner. The Barnett–Aden African–American Art Collection was developed in Washington in the 1940s. Of particular interest is the work of Lois Mailou Jones.

Location:	1305 North Florida Avenue
Hours:	Tuesday through Saturday, 10–4:30, Sunday 1–4:30, closed major holidays
Fees:	Adults $3, seniors over 65 and children 5–18 $2
Phone:	(813) 272–2466

Children enjoy the interactive exhibits at the *Museum of Science & Industry (MOSI)*. These exhibits tell about agriculture, environment, science, technology, health, industry, and weather. The weather exhibits are particularly interesting as you experience a simulated hurricane and learn about a thunderstorm as part of the Gulf Coast Hurricane. Major scientific phenomena are explained in Dr. Thunder's Magic Boom Room. This is a giant facility with more than 450 hands–on exhibits. We always head for the Saunders Planetarium when we're ready to sit down and be amazed.

Location:	4801 East Fowler Avenue
Hours:	Sunday through Thursday 9–5, Friday and Saturday 9–9
Fees:	**Combination Science Museum and MOSIMAX:** Adults $11, seniors over 50 and students with valid ID $9, children 2–12 $7. **Science Museum only:** Adults $ 8, seniors over 50 and students with valid ID $7, children 2–12 $5. **MOSIMAX only**: Adults $6, seniors over 50 and students with valid ID 5, children 2–12 $4
Phone:	(813) 987–6100

B*usch Gardens* is a 300 acre theme park which includes over 3,000 animals, from rare white Bengal tigers to African big game. At the Dark Continent there are 400 exotic big game which can be seen by monorail, steam locomotive, or sky ride. Then take a ride on the Congo River Rapids. It's fun! Particularly for those Southerners who rarely see ice, step into the Moroccan Palace Theatre. The ice show is particularly enjoyable on a hot day. Egypt, a seven acre area has a roller coaster, museum, and a dig site. There is a great deal to see and do. Come for a day, come back for several more!

Location:	3000 East Busch Boulevard at 40th Street
Hours:	Daily 9–7, plus seasonal extended hours
Fees:	Adults $38.45, children 3–9 $32, 2nd day admission $10.65
Phone:	(813) 987—5082

At the *Lowry Park Zoo,* two of our favorite exhibits are the free–flight aviary and the Pepsi Manatee and Aquatic Center which offers emergency care to injured or sick manatees. Watch their recovery process through large plate glass panels which provide underwater and surface viewing opportunities. If you have time, pause for a stroll through the botanical gardens.

Location:	7530 North Boulevard
Hours:	Daily 9:30–5, last admission at 4:45
Fees:	Adults 12-49 $7.50, seniors over 50 $6.50, children 3–11 $4.50
Phone:	(813) 935–8552

The *Florida Aquarium* is a virtual microcosm of Florida following the state's water story from its underground source through freshwater wetlands and estuaries, bays and beaches, coral reefs, and out to the open sea. Its more than 5,000 specimens are housed in a three story, shell–shaped, glass–domed building. This "fourth generation" aquarium is composed of four main exhibit galleries: Florida Wetlands, Florida Bays & Beaches, Florida Coral Reefs, and Florida Offshore. Be sure to find the spring that turns into a river, watch otters play, explore the cypress swamp, and pick your way back through the mangrove roots.

Location:	701 Channelside Drive
Hours:	Daily 9:30–5, closed Thanksgiving and Christmas
Fees:	Adults $13.95, seniors over 59 and students 13–18 $12.55, children 3–12 $6.95
Phone:	(813) 273–4020

Ybor City

When cigar-making employees in Key West wanted more money and better working conditions, several cigar manufacturers came to Tampa. Don Vincente Martinez Ybor, a political exile from Cuba, was one of them. He bought 40 acres of land and opened his Ybor City factory and housing for his workers in 1886. At one time, the Ybor factory was the largest cigar producing factory in the world and employed over 4,000 people.

Cigar makers, or tabaqueros as they were known, worked at long tables in double rows. While working, readers, or lectors, read to the workers—in the morning it would usually be political tracts; in the afternoon, literature. It was in the cigar factories of Ybor City that the importance of America's involvement in the Spanish–American War was discussed. This ultimately led to letters to the Federal government in Washington, D. C. and the battles that followed.

To learn more about the area's history, visit the **Ybor City State Museum** and the nearby **Cigar Workers' Homes**. The museum is housed in the renovated **Ferlita Bakery**, once a principal source of the community's daily bread. It provides a wonderful history of the growth of the area and of the cigar industry in Cuba and Ybor City. The **Cigar Workers' Homes** are frame cottages, typical of those once common in the community. They were built on a long, narrow Spanish–style floor plan that has rooms lined one behind the other opening off a long hallway to one side. They were referred to as conones, cannons, or shotgun houses since it was said that a shotgun could be fired from the front door to the back without hitting a wall. Two cottages display exhibits of cigar making history, one serves as a house museum.

Location:	1818 East Ninth Avenue
Hours:	Tuesday through Saturday 9–12 and 1–5. **Tours** : 10–12 and 1–3. Closed Thanksgiving and Christmas
Fees:	Adults and children over 6 $2
Phone:	(813) 247–6323

St. Petersburg

When Henry B. Plant's railroad was established in 1885, Peter Demens, another railroader, extended the Orange Belt Railroad. He named one of the stops after St. Petersburg, his home city in Russia. Senior citizens began arriving in the late 1800s, soon after a national medical association commented that St. Petersburg was one of the best and healthiest places to retire.

The young at heart of all ages gather at the *Coliseum Ballroom*, known as the Mediterranean Revival Palace of Pleasure when the dance hall opened in 1924. This is the place to go if you love to dance to the big band sound. Picture yourself in a 15,500 square foot room, with a highly polished red oak dance floor. So, dress in your favorite 1920s outfit. Choose a partner and step onto the dance floor for a twirl into yesterday.

Location:	535 Fourth Avenue North
Hours:	**Tea Dances:** Wednesdays from 1–3:30
Fees:	General admission: $4
Phone:	(813) 892–5202

To understand more about the area, visit the *St. Petersburg Museum of History*. One especially interesting area is the Benoist Pavillion. It tells the story of the start of commercial aviation when, in 1914, Tony Jannus piloted the first commercial flight ever between St. Petersburg and Tampa.

Location:	335 Second Avenue Northeast
Hours:	Monday through Saturday 10–5, Sunday 1–5, closed major holidays
Fees:	Adults $4, seniors over 62 and college students $3.50, children 7–17 $1.50
Phone:	(813) 894–1052

When visiting *The Museum of Fine Arts*, be sure to see the French impressionist paintings including works by Monet and Renoir. There are also remarkable photography, pre–Columbian, and Steuben glass collections. There are also fine period rooms and lovely gardens for reflecting on the beauty of the art.

Location:	255 Beach Drive Northeast at Second Avenue
Hours:	Tuesday through Saturday 10–5, Sunday 1–5, third Thursday 10–9. **Tours**: Tuesday through Friday: 10, 11, 1, and 2. Saturday: 11,1, and 2. Sunday 1 and 2. Closed major holidays
Fees:	Adults $6, seniors over 65 $3, students $2. No charge on Sundays
Phone:	(813) 896–2667

One of the city's best known museums is the *Salvador Dali Museum*. It houses the largest private collection of the famous Spanish surrealist artist's works with more than 1,000 pieces. The collection was assembled over a 40 year period by A. Reynolds and Eleanor Morse who wintered in St. Petersburg and worked closely with the artist as they planned the museum. Plan to join one of the tours conducted in the gallery and, we expect, you will particularly enjoy learning about the large paintings on the far walls.

Location:	1000 Third Street South
Hours:	Monday through Saturday 9:30–5:30, Sunday 12–5:30. Closed Thanksgiving and Christmas
Fees:	Adults $8, seniors over 65 $7, students 10 and older $4. **Tours**: Daily
Phone:	(813) 823–3767

Go through the 90 foot Touch Tunnel maze in the dark at the *Great Explorations* hands–on science museum. Great for kids! A few of the other outstanding exhibits include Explore Galore for the under–7 set and Think Tank, a puzzleville for somewhat older children. Children and parents both enjoy Body Shop to learn more about health and fitness.

Location:	1120 Fourth Street South
Hours:	Monday through Saturday 10–5, Sunday 12– 5. Closed major holidays
Fees:	Adults $6, seniors over 66 $5.50, children 3–17 $5
Phone:	(813) 821–8992 or 8885

Experience a trip between St. Petersburg and Sarasota by driving across the ***Sunshine Skyway Bridge***. A 4.1 mile span, the bridge is a work of art which crosses Tampa Bay on Highway 275. The design of the suspension bridge catches the light and reminds us of an aerial sailboat.

Sunshine Skyway Bridge

The Ringling Museum of Art

in Sarasota

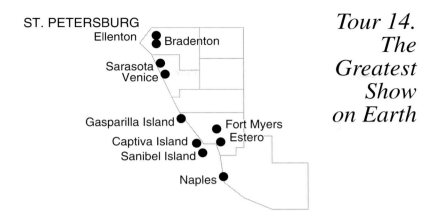

ST. PETERSBURG

Ellenton Bradenton

Sarasota
Venice

Gasparilla Island   Fort Myers
Captiva Island   Estero
Sanibel Island

Naples

*Tour 14.
The
Greatest
Show
on Earth*

Allow plenty of time when visiting this beautiful part of the coast. Explorers, plantations, pirates, circus folk, and inventors all await your visit.

The Greatest Show on Earth's winter headquarters were in Sarasota and then in Venice. We visit the American palace and art museum created by John and Mable Ringling, part of a great circus family.

Meanwhile, just down the coast at Fort Myers, Thomas Alva Edison and Henry Ford, two of the great inventors of our time, were at work in their winter laboratories revolutionizing American industry.

Ellenton

Ellenton was a Confederate stronghold during the Civil War. The **Gamble Plantation State Historic Site** and **Memorial to J. P. Benjamin** are located on land that was formerly a sugar plantation and refinery covering 3,500 acres. The house is the only antebellum plantation that has survived in South Florida. It was built in the late 1840s by Robert Gamble, a banker and Confederate major.

Slaves made bricks of broken shell and mortar for the walls. The plaster was a mix of sand, lime, and sugar. Since sugar was raised on the plantation, it was the least expensive binding agent available. It held very well. In addition to the plantation house, look for the ruins of the sugar mill. At the time of the Civil War, this was one of the largest mills in the South. Confederate Secretary of State Judah P. Benjamin was sheltered in the plantation house after the fall of the Confederacy. He hid here until safe passage to England could be arranged. The monument has been erected in his honor.

Location:	3708 Patten Avenue
Hours:	**Park**: Daily 8–sunset. **Tours**: Thursday through Monday at 9:30, 10:30, 1, 2, 3, and 4. Buy your ticket as soon as you arrive, because tours sell out quickly
Fees:	**Park**: No charge. **Tours**: Adults $3, children 6–12 $1.50
Phone:	(941) 723–4536

Bradenton

Life was hard for the early settlers. The *Manatee Village Historical Park* makes it easier to understand the lives of early Florida pioneers who lived in the area from

Early settlers, ca. 1895

1841–1914. Six historic buildings, dating from 1860 to 1912, were moved to the site and can be toured. They include a courthouse, a church, a farm, a store, a schoolhouse, and a home. Children enjoy the room in the Wiggins Store where they can dress up in period costumes, play with toys from the early part of the century, and imagine life as a child in those days.

Location:	604 15th Street East
Hours:	**September through June**: Monday through Friday 9–4:30, Sunday 1:30–4:30. **July and August**: Monday through Friday 9–4:30. Closed holidays. **Tours**: September through May: 9:30–3:30
Fees:	No charge, donations welcome
Phone:	(941) 741–4076

In 1539, Hernando De Soto and 600 of his men landed near the site of today's ***De Soto National Memorial***. They were searching for gold. For four years they looked in what are now Georgia, South Carolina, North Carolina, Tennessee, Alabama, Mississippi, and Texas, but found no treasure. The soldiers stole food from the Indians and brought numerous diseases to the New World for which the Indians had no immunity. During this time, almost 300 members of the expedition died, including De Soto in 1542 in what is present day Arkansas. Luis de Moscoso then took command. He tried to lead the remaining troops to Mexico by going overland through Texas. That didn't work. They returned to the Mississippi, built boats, and reached Mexico by water in 1543.

Make your first stop the Visitor Center which has an excellent film describing the expedition. While there, pause to look at the small replica of one of De Soto's ships and an excellent collection of 16th–century armor, weaponry, and other military artifacts. It's hard to imagine the soldiers wearing or carrying such heavy gear through the Florida swamps. There is also a half–mile, self–guided nature trail through a mangrove forest. The memorial provides an appreciation of the scope of DeSoto's explorations. It was the first intensive exploratory effort in our nation's interior. A great deal of knowledge of the lands and peoples was gained despite great hardship and the continuing frustration of not finding any treasure. However, the De Soto expedition may have given rise to further exploration and the eventual settlement of what is now the United States.

Location:	75th Street Northwest
Hours:	**Park:** Daily sunrise to sunset. **Visitor Center**: Daily 9–5. Closed Thanksgiving, Christmas, and New Year's Day. **History Camp**: Late December through Easter: Wednesday through Sunday at 11, 12:30, 2, and 3:30
Fees:	No charge
Phone:	(941) 792–0458

Learn about Florida from prehistoric to Space Age times at the ***South Florida Museum, Bishop Planetarium, and Parker Aquarium***. There is a life–size diorama showing how area Indians lived. A statue of Hernando De Soto is in the middle of a tile fountain in the Spanish Plaza, as is a 16th–century Spanish chapel, and a white stucco copy of De Soto's birthplace in Spain. Moving to the 60,000 gallon aquarium, meet Snooty, the manatee, and learn about Florida's environment. The Bishop Observatory has a roll-back–domed ceiling with a six inch refracting telescope. We urge you to stop to see the 1927 Model T Ford and think about gas costing a whopping 15.5¢ a gallon.

Location:	201 Tenth Street West
Hours:	**Museum**: Tuesday through Saturday 10–5, Sunday 12–5 and Mondays January through April and July. **Planetarium**: Starshows 1 and 4. **Laser Show:** 2:30. In addition, there are evening planetarium, observatory, and laser programs. Please phone for details and schedules.
Fees:	**Museum, Planetarium, and Aquarium**: Adults $6, seniors over 60 $5, children 5–12 $3.50. **Evening Planetarium Starshow and Observatory:** Adults $3, children $1.50. **Observatory Alone:** $1. **Evening Laser Shows:** Adults $5.50, children $3.50
Phone:	(941) 746–4132

Sarasota

Pioneer settlement of the area began in the 1840s. Bertha Potter Palmer, a Chicago millionaire, "discovered" Sarasota in 1910. She bought 140,000 acres of land because she thought the area was more beautiful than the Bay of Naples. Largely due to her promotion of the area, Sarasota's tourist industry was born.

The next millionaire to significantly impact Sarasota was John Ringling. He made the city the winter hub of the Ringling Bros. Circus and became a major land owner in the area. In addition, John and Mable Ringling created an outstanding art collection.

By the early 1920s, they began designing a home and a museum to hold their vast art collection. In 1926, they built *Ca'd'Zan*, the House of John. It cost $1.5 million—plus furnishings. It has 30 rooms and 14 baths. The windows are set with handmade Venetian tinted glass. The home is one of Florida's most elaborate palaces built during the period. Walk to the Sarasota Bay side of the home to appreciate the architecture and craftsmanship.

The Ringlings were very much involved in the design of their home and incorporated design elements from the Italian and French Renaissance as well as Baroque, Venetian Gothic, and Modern periods in the architectural design. Look carefully at the period furnishings and art. Then step into the ballroom or the game room to note the ceiling panels painted by Willy Pogany, set designer for the Ziegfeld Follies.

John Ringling, ca. 1905

Photo courtesy of Ringling Bros. and
Barnum & Bailey Combined Shows, Inc.

The *John and Mable Ringling Museum of Art,* completed in 1929, is known throughout the world for its rich and varied collection including Old Masters, Late Medieval, and Renaissance works. At his death, John Ringling willed the house, grounds, and museum to Florida and the facility is now known as the *State Museum of Florida*.

The *Asolo Theater* is also on the property. It is a restored 19th–century Italian theater with ornate panels and an interesting story of its "rediscovery" and purchase.

Step right up! In 1948, two years after assuming ownership of the Museum, the State of Florida honored the Ringlings by establishing the *Circus Galleries.* Walk inside to see circus wagons, photographs of circus personalities, rare circus lithographs, posters, and a scale model of a three–ring circus. The museum was built in the image of a 19th–century Parisian circus amphitheater.

Location:	5401 Bayshore Road, US Highway 41
Hours:	**Museums**: Daily 10–5:30. Closed major holidays
Fees:	**Gardens**: No charge. **Buildings:** Adults and children over 13 $8.50, seniors over 62 $7.50, Florida students and teachers with ID: No charge. **Art Museum Only**: Saturdays no charge
Phone:	(941) 359–5700

Beauty lives at the *Marie Selby Botanical Gardens* and its fine collection of epiphytes (air plants) from the tropics. The highlight of a visit is a chance to see the outstanding orchid collection, perhaps the most beautiful collection of orchids at any botanical garden in the U.S. While here, make time to tour the historic *Payne Mansion* which houses the *Museum of Botany and the Arts.* Baywalk Sanctuary provides a leisurely walk through an interesting mangrove swamp. We also enjoy visiting the display greenhouse.

Location:	811 South Palm Avenue
Hours:	Daily 10–5. Closed Christmas
Fees:	Adults $7, children 6–11 $3
Phone:	(941) 366–5730

Listen to sounds in the Echo Chamber and freeze a shadow. Experiment with static electricity and take apart a telephone. Although primarily designed as a hands–on museum for children, the *Gulf Coast World of Science* is an interesting spot for youngsters of all ages. Children always enjoy the bubble machine!

Location:	8251 15th Street East at the Airport Mall
Hours:	Tuesday through Saturday 10–5, Sunday 1–5, closed major holidays
Fees:	Adults $3, children over 2, $1.50
Phone:	(941) 359–9975

Visit Florida's largest state park. *Myakka River State Park* has over 28,000 acres of river, lakes, marsh, hammocks, and prairie and is one of the country's outstanding wildlife sanctuaries and breeding grounds. We suggest that you take the five mile drive through part of the park to acquaint you with its overall features. The paved road along the Myakka River and Upper Myakka Lake is several miles long and good for biking. Binoculars or a telescope are recommended for birding and the great views across the marsh and river. Although tram tours and air boat rides begin at the boat basin, biking and canoeing are also wonderful ways to see the area. About 200 species of birds have been spotted in the park. The area is best hiked in the dry season—late fall and early spring. There are the remains of pioneer settlements and old cattle camps to be discovered.

Location:	9 miles East of I–75 on Hwy 72
Hours:	**Park:** Daily, 8–sunset. **Tram Tours:** December through May. **Air Boat Tours: December 15 through May:** Daily at 11:30,1, and 2:30. **June through December 14:** Daily at 10, 11:30, and 1.
Fees:	**Park:** $4 per vehicle with 2–8 passengers, $2 for one person in a vehicle, $1 for bikers. **Air Boat or Tram Tour:** Adults $7, children 6–12 $3
Phone:	(941) 361–6511

Sarasota Bay

The *Mote Marine Aquarium* and *Ann and Alfred Goldstein Marine Mammal Research and Rehabilitation Center* is exceptional. Be sure to see the 135,000 gallon outdoor Shark Tank and the manatee exhibit with two captive born manatees. There are over 20 aquaria containing over 200 varieties of fish and invertebrate sea creatures. The facility also includes a Science Center. Be captivated by the Grassflat Exhibit in a pool about the size of a small dinner table and about waist–high. Small fish dart around the grasses nibbling at floating bits of food. Before leaving, we always pause to enjoy the setting by looking out over Sarasota and the Bay. Ninety–minute sea life boat tours are offered. Travel into Sarasota Bay past a bird rookery (bring your binoculars). The boat then docks on an uninhabited island for a brief nature walk, and returns by way of trolling the sea bass beds.

Location:	1600 Ken Thompson Parkway
Hours:	**Aquarium:** Daily 10–5. **Boat Tours::** 11. 1:30, and 3:30. Closed Thanksgiving, Christmas, and Easter
Fees:	**Aquarium:** Adults $8, children 4–17, $6. **Boat:** Adults $24, children 5–17 $20. **Combination Ticket:** Adults $28, children $22
Phone:	**Aquarium:** (941) 388–2451 or (800) 691 MOTE **Boat Tours:** (941) 388–4200

Longboat Key

Injured pelicans have been known to find their way to the *Pelican Man's Bird Sanctuary*. Birds that can be rehabilitated are then released. For those birds which are too damaged or ill to be returned to the wild, there is an aviary in the sanctuary.

Location:	1708 Ken Thompson Parkway
Hours:	Daily 10–5, closed major holidays
Fees:	No charge, donations welcome
Phone:	(941) 388–4444

Venice/Venice Beach

During the land boom of the 1920s, the Brotherhood of Locomotive Engineers came to Florida to find land for a town. John Nolan, an eminent town planner was hired. Small farms and residential lots were laid out. Business and industrial districts were also designed to be part of the 30,000 acre plot. Venice was the result. The land boom collapsed in the late 1920s and, by 1930, all but a handful of residents had departed.

People interested in shark teeth and fossils comb the sands at Venice Beach. Because the beach is near the longest sloping continental shelf in the world, this is a particularly good spot to go fossil hunting. Some of the teeth being washed ashore belong to creatures that have been extinct for millions of years. Bring a scoop and start looking in the sand in shallow water.

North Port

The springs at **Warm Mineral Springs and Cyclorama** produce nine million gallons daily at a constant water temperature of 87 degrees. It is an unexpected treat to cool off here. The Cyclorama is a rotunda 226 feet in diameter. It is lined with murals showing Ponce de León's varied and interesting adventures.

Location:	12200 San Servando Avenue
Hours:	**Springs:** Daily 9–5. Closed Christmas. **Cyclorama:** Daily at 1
Fees:	Adults $7, children 12–18 $4.50, children 2–11 $2
Phone:	(941) 426–1692

Gasparilla Island

In the 1780s, a cultivated, well–dressed, well–read Spanish pirate assembled a band of cutthroats. He established a base on an island he named Gasparilla—after himself. In 1801, he captured Maria Louisa, a Spanish princess. A year earlier she had gone to Mexico with eleven beautiful, young Mexican noblewomen. They were all sailing back to Spain where the Mexican girls were to be educated. Gasparilla struck their vessel off the coast of Boca Grande. He killed the crew, took the gold, and carried the young women to nearby Captiva Island, hence one of many legends began about the island's name. Gasparilla terrorized ship captains and passengers until 1822 when his boat was boarded. Rather than be captured, he tied an anchor around his waist, leaped into the water, and drowned.

Fort Myers

Fort Myers was a military outpost during the Seminole Indian Wars and was then abandoned. Thomas Alva Edison came to Fort Myers in 1886. He was 39 years old, ill, and trying to regain his health. He succeeded—and spent winters in Fort Myers until his death at the age of 84. He was one of its more famous winter residents and was one of the city's great promoters. In 1900, he imported 200 royal palms from Cuba to "dress up" the look of the city.

Thomas Alva Edison, 1847–1931. Mr. Edison was one of the most prolific inventors of all time, and held 1,097 patents. He is best known for the invention of the incandescent lamp and the development of the electrical industry. Some of his other inventions created the phonograph, moving picture, telegraph, and telephone industries. Many feel that he is the person who has had the most profound effect on the development of the modern world.

Thomas Alva and Mina Edison's two story frame home on the Caloosahatchee River is Victorian with gingerbread ornamentation. The swimming pool was reinforced with bamboo instead of steel and is filled by an artesian well 1,100 feet deep. Edison drew the plans for the house himself. In 1885, it was built in sections in Fairfield, Maine. They were shipped to Fort Myers in four sailing ships and the house was assembled in 1886. He planted more than a thousand varieties of plants imported from all over the world in his tropical botanical garden. You won't be able to miss the banyan tree in the parking area at the *Edison–Ford Winter Estate.* The banyon tree was two inches in diameter in 1925 when Edison's friend and Fort Myers neighbor Harvey Firestone brought it to him from India. Wonderful tours are provided showing both the *Edison Winter Home, Gardens, and Museum* and the *Henry Ford Winter Home*.

While working in his Fort Myers laboratory, he perfected and patented the teletype, the phonograph, motion pictures, and other inventions. His laboratory contains the original equipment used for much of his research from 1925 to 1931. When he had perfected the electric lamp, Mr. Edison offered to install free lights in the town, provided the residents would supply the poles and wires. The town council rejected the proposal because they felt the lights might keep the cattle awake. True story!

One of Mr. Edison's treasured gifts was an early Model T automobile given to him by his friend and neighbor, Henry Ford. Every year, Henry Ford offered him a new car in exchange for his "old" car. Mr. Edison liked his own car and refused the offer each year. So, since Henry Ford couldn't give his friend a new car, he did the next best thing.

At the start of each winter season, Henry Ford, his mechanics, and boxes of auto parts arrived at the Fort Myers train station. In this way, new improvements were hand–tooled into Mr. Edison's car.

The *Henry Ford Winter Home, Mangoes,* is next door to the Edison home. The Fords bought the simple frame house in

1916, just four years after mass production of the Model T began in Detroit. They wanted to live next door to their friends, Mina and Thomas Alva Edison. Henry Ford and his family spent many winters here. He often went across the lawn to work with his neighbor in Edison's laboratory. It is interesting to note that the Fords never returned to the home after their good friend and neighbor, Thomas Edison, died in 1931. After Mrs. Ford's death, the furnishings in the house were sold. Years later the house was refurnished to reflect the 1920s period.

Location:	2350 McGregor Boulevard
Hours:	Monday through Saturday 9–5;30, Sunday 12–5:30, closed Thanksgiving and Christmas. **Tours**: Throughout the day lasting about 80 minutes. The last complete tour (Edison and Ford Estates) departs at 3:30. An Edison Estate only tour departs at 4.
Fees:	**Combined Tour:** Adults $10, children 6–12 $5. **Edison Tour at 4 pm:** Adults $8, children 6–12 $4
Phone:	(941) 334–7419

For a glimpse of Southwest Florida, visit the *Fort Myers Historical Museum*, housed in a 1924 railroad depot. As you arrive, look at the private railroad car. The Esperanza Pullman Car provides a look at the way the wealthy once traveled to Florida. The car is almost 84 feet long and 11 feet wide. There is a lounge, three staterooms and a master suite, a dining room, kitchen, pantry, and porter's room. There is also a P–39 bomber which was excavated from Estero Bay. Step inside to see the Calusa Indian exhibit, information about early pioneer and agricultural history, and the replica of a Florida Cracker's home. Watch for a major interactive baseball exhibit showing the history of baseball in Lee County— winter home to six major league teams at various times.

Location:	2300 Peck Street
Hours:	Tuesday through Saturday 9–4:30. Closed major holidays
Fees:	Adults $2.50, children 2–11 $1
Phone:	(941) 332–5955

For a fun day with the children, plan a visit to the 105–acre *Calusa Nature Center of Lee County and Planetarium.* Visit the Audubon Aviary, a sugar press, and an outdoor bobcat exhibit.

There is also an Indian Village showing how the Seminole and Calusa Indians lived. The live snake exhibit is popular with children! Everyone enjoys a walk along the nature trails.

Location:	3450 Ortiz Avenue
Hours:	**Nature Center:** Monday through Saturday 9–5, Sunday 11–5. **Planetarium**: Wednesday through Saturday, times vary. **Laser Show**: Friday and Saturday nights, times vary. Call for schedule.
Fees:	**Nature Center**: Adults $4, children 3–12 $2.50 **Planetarium**: Adults $3, children 3–12 $2. **Laser Show**: General Admission $5
Phone:	(941) 275–3435

Sanibel Island

Sanibel's beach is considered one of the three best shelling beaches in the world. The other two are in Africa and the southwest Pacific. If you search for shells, be prepared to go home with a back condition known as the *Sanibel Stoop*. To increase your knowledge and the quality of your selections, pick up a guide to Florida shells. Plan to search after storms, at and after high tide, and early in the morning. This beautiful island was named by Ponce de León in 1513. He called it Costa de Caracoles, the Coast of Seashells. Besides beach walking, try exploring by bicycle from April through September when the roads are relatively empty.

Bailey–*Matthews Shell Museum* tells the story of life of sea shells and their conservation. The museum features shells from around the world and information about their use throughout history. A new Children's Room features a touch tank.

Location:	3075 Sanibel–Captiva Road
Hours:	Tuesday through Sunday 10–4
Fees:	Adults $5, children 7-18 $3
Phone:	(941) 395–2233

The *J.N. "Ding" Darling National Wildlife Refuge* was established in 1945 to commemorate one of Florida's early and important environmentalists and political cartoonists. The natural place to begin a visit to this exceptional facility is the Visitor's Center. If a tour is scheduled, join it. Otherwise, travel slowly along the five mile auto drive through the mangrove forest and along the waterways. This wilderness is a way station for migrating ducks and shelters more than 200 varieties of birds. Viewing is best at sunrise or sunset. Bring binoculars. Watch for the brilliantly colored roseate spoonbills and woodstorks. It is also recommended that you make time for the nature trail walkway or just paddle along the winding canoe trails in this 54,000 acre refuge. It is a beautiful spot to watch for birds, wildlife, and natural beauty.

Roseate Spoonbills

Location:	One Wildlife Drive
Hours:	**Refuge**: Saturday through Thursday sunrise to sunset. **Visitor Center**: **Early November through mid–April**, Monday through Thursday, Saturday and Sunday 9–5; Balance of Year: Monday through Thursday, Saturday and Sunday 9–4. **Wildlife Drive:** Saturday through Thursday sunrise to sunset. Closed major holidays
Fees:	$4 per car and its riders, $1 for bicyclists or hikers
Phone:	(941) 472–1100

Captiva Island

Although the island's name was attributed to Gasparilla's holding women captive on the island, the name was actually listed on maps long before he arrived in the area. For many years, the island housed the country's largest key lime plantation. Especially on Captiva Island, it seems important to relax and let island time— the natural rhythm of tides and storms, sunrises and sunsets—take over. Many years ago, Anne Morrow Lindbergh visited Captiva Island and was inspired to write *A Gift from the Sea*.

Estero

The remains of an unusual pioneer settlement are pre-served on the banks of the Estero River. Koreshan Unity was formed in Chicago by Cyrus Teed, a religious visionary, in 1886. With his followers, he moved to this site in 1894 to build a New Jerusalem. The remains of his community is part of the ***Koreshan State Historic Site*** and ***Mound Key State Architectural Site.*** With high ceilings and pitched roofs, the 11 remaining buildings reflect a practical approach to the subtropical climate. The furnishings were brought from Chicago and are late 19th–century Victorian. Members of the community believed the earth was a hollow sphere with all life, planets, moon, and stars within it. After Cyrus Teed died in 1908, membership declined quickly. By 1961, the four remaining members deeded the land to the State of Florida.

Location:	Corner of US 41 at Corkscrew Road
Hours:	**Park**: 8–sunset. **Historic Site**: Daily 8–5
	Ranger Tours: Saturday and Sunday at 1
Fees:	**Park:** $3.25 per car, with up to 8 people per vehicle, $1 for hikers or bicyclists. **Tours:** Adults $1, children 6–11 50¢
Phone:	(941) 992–0311

Naples

Naples is a wonderful community to explore by bicycle or by foot. This is one of our favorite parts of the state for bird watching.

Southwest Florida's subtropical ecosystems are high-lighted at the ***Naples Nature Center.*** There are hands–on exhib-its, video presentations, and special programs. Make time to visit the state–of–the–art hospital at the Wildlife Rehabilitation Center to learn about wild animal rehabilitation. Recuperating wildlife can be observed through special on–line monitors. Florida Coast to Coast provides hands–on activities bringing to life how water flows across the state—and its importance. And thinking of water, make arrangements to take a free guided boat tour or rent a canoe or kayak and travel along the self–guided Aquatic Trail.

Location:	14th Avenue North, off Goodlette–Frank Road
Hours:	**January through March:** Monday through Saturday 9–4:30, Sunday 1–5. **April through December:** Monday through Saturday 9–4:30
Fees:	Adults $5, children 5–17 $1. **Boat Tour:** no charge. **Canoe and Kayak Rentals:** Two hours $13
Phone:	(941) 775–8569

Walk along a half–mile boardwalk to see Florida's vanishing scrub, look at the juvenile alligators in the large aquariums, and visit the Butterfly Garden at the *Briggs Nature Center*. This is also a fantastic birding location since it is located in the 12,700 acre *Rookery Bay National Estuarine Research Reserve*.

Location:	401 Shell Road, six miles North of Marco Island
Hours:	Monday through Friday 9–4:30. **January through March**: Additional Hours 1–5 Sunday. **October through May:** Monday through Saturday 9–4:30.,
Fees:	**Boardwalk:** Adults $3, children 3–17 $1 **Butterfly Garden, Interpretive Center:** No charge **Canoe and Kayak Rentals:** Two hours $13
Phone:	(941) 262–0304

Corkscrew Swamp Wildlife Sanctuary is one of the beautiful Florida Audubon wildlife sanctuaries and a major bird watching site. Amble along the two and a quarter mile boardwalk which loops through the sanctuary. It is the only access permitted to the area. The walk passes through pine forest, wet prairie, cypress forest, swamp, hammock, and marsh. For the best viewing of the wood storks, visit between December and March when they nest and breed. The bald cypress stand is said to be the largest in the country. The trees are large and some are over 500 years old.

Location:	County Road 846, then left on Sanctuary Road
Hours:	**December to May:** Daily 7–5. **November through April:** Daily 8–5
Fees:	Adults $6.50, college students $5, children 6–18 $3,
Phone:	(941) 657–3771

Tarpon Springs Fisherman
Threading Sponges,
May 1944

Cedar Key ●

Homosassa Springs ●

Brooksville ●
Masaryktown ●

Tarpon Springs ●
Indian Shores ●
Clearwater ●
Largo ●

● TAMPA

Tour 15.
Time
Lapse
Territory

The farther north you travel on this tour, the more the area begins to resemble the Florida of the early 20th–century. Travel to some of the state's oldest sponge beds and then through hardwood forests to Cedar Key, once the other end of the rail line that began on Amelia Island. Cedar Key, with its bayous, turn–of– the–century dwellings, and uneasy truce with hurricanes, provides a look at the survival of a naturally beautiful part of Florida.

Clearwater

Henry Plant was the west coast's railroading and tourism entrepreneur. He believed in Clearwater and established a railroad station and the ***Belleview Biltmore Hotel.*** Opening in 1897, the hotel became a major tourist resort. The 365 room hotel remains the largest occupied wooden structure in the world. In the 1940s, the entire hotel was used by the U.S. Army as a barracks. The building has been beautifully restored. Antiques, Queen Anne furnishings, and stories are featured in the tour through this classic turn–of–the–century building.

Location:	25 Belleview Boulevard
Hours:	**Tour**: Daily at 11 am
Fees:	**Tour:** Adults $5, children 12-17 $3. **Tour and Luncheon:** Adults $13.50
Phone:	(813) 442–6171

The ***Clearwater Aquarium and Marine Science Center*** has live and model displays of area marine life. Be sure to see the sea turtle and dolphin tanks as well as the touch tanks. The facility, one of only eight in the nation, is committed to the rescue, treatment, and release of marine mammals and sea turtles.

Location:	249 Windward Passage
Hours:	Monday through Friday 9–5, Saturday 9–4, Sunday 11–4. Closed major holidays
Fees:	Adults $6.75, children 3–12 $4.25
Phone:	(813) 441–1790

If you're ready for a change of scene and an outdoor adventure, visit *Moccasin Lake Nature Center and Park*. It is an environmental and energy education center. The nature trail through hardwood and wetlands is just about perfect for an afternoon hike. The interpretive center provides interesting background on the setting and the wildlife you may see. This location also serves as a refuge for permanently injured birds of prey that are native to Florida.

Location:	2750 Park Trail Lane
Hours:	Tuesday through Friday 9–5, Saturday and Sunday 10–6. Closed major holidays
Fees:	Adults $2, children 3–12, $1
Phone:	(813) 462–6024 or 6417

Caladesi Island/Honeymoon Island

In 1830, there was a single barrier island named Sand Island. Fifty years later, its name was changed to Hog Island. In 1921, a hurricane split the barrier island into two. Eighteen years later, a New York developer acquired the land for $30,000. He wanted the beautiful barrier island to sound attractive and renamed one of the islands Honeymoon Island. He built palm–thatched bungalows and advertised it as a tropical honeymoon resort. Today, *Honeymoon Island State Park* can be reached by cause-way. There is a hiking trail along the northern loop. This is the site of one of only a few virgin slash pine stands in south Florida and is an important nesting site for osprey.

The second barrier island was named Caladesi. Today, *Caladesi Island State Park* has one of the most beautiful natural beaches in the world and a wonderful hiking trail. This is one of the state's few undeveloped barrier islands. Watch for armadillos, marsh rabbits, birds, and flowering plants along the nature trail.

Location:	**Honeymoon Island:** Accessible by causeway off the Gulf Coast from 586, north of Clearwater. **Caladesi Island:** Accessible by ferry from Honeymoon Island.
Hours:	Daily 8–sunset
Fees:	**Park entrance fees**: **Honeymoon**: $4 per vehicle for car and up to eight people, $1 for hikers and bikers. **Caladesi:** By private boat, entrance fee is $3.25 for day use. **Ferry Fee:** Adults $4, children 3–12 $2.50.
Phone:	(813) 469–5918

Largo

There is an excellent photography collection showing the lives of the area's pioneers at the *Heritage Village—Pinellas County Historical Museum.* While thinking about the pioneers, walk through part of the 21 acre site that shows lifestyles from the turn-of-the-century. Over a dozen historically significant buildings have been assembled to reconstruct the area's setting as it might have been.

Location:	11909 125th Street North
Hours:	Tuesday through Saturday 10–4, Sunday 1–4, closed national holidays
Fees:	No charge, donations welcome
Phone:	(813) 582–2123

Indian Shores

Suncoast Seabird Sanctuary is a refuge and rehabilitation center for injured wild birds. Opened in the early 1970s, the Sanctuary now cares for up to 500 birds at a time.

Location:	18328 Gulf Boulevard
Hours:	Daily 9–sunset. **Educational Programs:** Tuesdays at 2 and the first Sunday of the month
Fees:	No charge, donations welcome
Phone:	(813) 391–6211

Tarpon Springs

The town, founded in 1876, was named in the mistaken belief that tarpon spawned in the nearby Spring Bayou. Shortly after its founding, a small group of Greek fishermen settled in the area to harvest sponge. They worked near shore and used the old country techniques of hooking sponges with long poles in shallow water. In the early 20th–century, deep sea diving equipment was developed. Although there was a lot of trial and error, the advances were watched with interest and, in 1905, the Tarpon Springs sponge divers began using deep sea diving gear. Wearing copper-helmeted diving suits, they were able to work far out at sea harvesting the rich sponge beds. As the equipment was perfected, so was Tarpon Springs' hold on the industry. Synthetic sponges had not yet been invented. Natural sponge harvesting became a multimillion dollar business. Unfortunately, the sponge industry collapsed in the 1950s due to two events: a red tide disease which harmed the sponge beds, and the introduction and rapid acceptance of synthetic sponges.

Although most of the divers' finds have been sponges, occasionally they bring other treasures to the surface. In 1938, a local sponge diver, Sozon Vatikiosis, brought in two seashells of previously unknown varieties. They were sent to the Smithsonian Institution and were later described as tea–rose blossoms which had turned to stone. The shells were named in honor of the diver and his wife and became part of the Smithsonian's permanent collection. It is interesting to wonder under what conditions and where these beautiful roses had bloomed, and when and how they were turned into such exquisite seashells.

St. Nicholas Greek Orthodox Cathedral was built in 1943 during the height of the Tarpon Springs' economic growth. It is a fine example of neo–Byzantine architecture. The icons, stained glass, and Grecian marble are particularly beautiful.

Location:	30 North Pinellas Avenue
Hours:	**Office:** Monday through Friday, 9-5. **Services:** Sunday 8, 9:30, and 11:30
Fees:	No charge, donations welcome
Phone:	(813) 937–3540

In 1918 a strong hurricane blew out the stained glass in the arched windows of the small *Unitarian Universalist Church*. Mrs.

George Inness, Jr. volunteered the services of her artist husband to paint wooden panels to fill the gaps. He created magnificent religious paintings. These, and additional works by Mr. Inness, are in place throughout the quiet sanctuary. George Inness, Jr. had studied in France and Italy. His style was quite similar to that of his father, a famous American landscape artist.

Location:	230 Grand Boulevard
Hours:	Tuesday through Sunday afternoons 2–5. Sunday services 10:30
Fees:	No charge, donations welcome
Phone:	(813) 937–4682

Brooksville

Look around the center of town. In the 1870s, there were no paved roads. The superhighway of its day was known as a Corduroy Road. It was made by paving trails with logs so the stage coaches could travel above the mud. One of these "superhighways" was the route used by the stage which raced through Brooksville on the way between Gainesville and Tampa.

Cedar Key

The area was settled in the early 1840s and became a thriving port city. Goods were shipped by water. Then, with the development of the cross–state railroad, cotton, lumber, and naval stores traveled by rail to Amelia Island and then north and east.

Unfortunately, the boom did not last. During the Civil War, blockade runners brought food and war materials for the Confederacy to Cedar Key's port. Salt, needed by the Southern armies, was made locally by boiling and evaporating sea water in large iron basins. The Unionists were aware of these activities. In 1862, a Union force attacked by sea, captured Cedar Key, and brought a halt to its then war–based economy.

After the war, the townspeople turned to timber. Pine and cypress were cut and shipped, cedar was and still is used to manufacture pencils. As the natural timber reserves began to be depleted in the 1880s, the area's residents turned to commercial fishing—which is still done on a small scale. However, today's Cedar Key has an uneasy economy which is largely dependent on fishing and tourism.

The *Cedar Key Historical Society Museum* shows the town's history dating back to the early 1800s. The collection is housed in an 1871 residence. Particular emphasis is placed on the pencil, lumber, and seafood industries.

Location:	609 Second Street at the courner with Route 24
Hours:	**May through October:** Sunday through Thursday 2–5, Friday and Saturday 11-5 **November through April:** Monday through Saturday 11–5, Sunday 2–4
Fees:	Adults $1, children 6–12 50¢
Phone:	(352) 543–5549

The visitor center at the *Cedar Key State Museum* contains exhibits which depict the colorful history of the area's growth as well as its natural history.

Location:	1710 Museum Drive
Hours:	Thursday through Monday 9–5
Fees:	Adults and children over 12 $1, children 6–12 50¢
Phone:	(352) 543–5350

Oysters are important

in Appalachicola and

along the Gulf Coast

Gulf
Coast
Florida

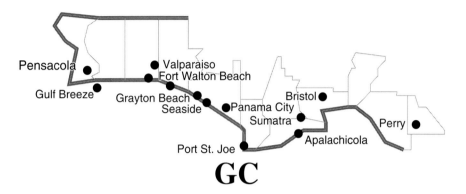

GC

The Florida Panhandle covers a vast area of land. You soon discover that the Gulf Coast portion of the Panhandle has historic cities, woods, wetlands, refuges, and magnificent beaches.

Throughout Florida's early constitutional history, various political and economic factions held strong views regarding how involved Florida should be with the United States. In Tour 16, the *Start of Statehood*, you travel to the site where all of the differences were resolved—at least for a short time.

Florida has many riches, among them are some of the most beautiful beaches in the world. Most longtime residents have a favorite beach and would be happy if no one else ever found it. Thus, a dilemma develops when it comes to talking about beaches. Whatever your personal choice, spend some time at the *Extraordinary Beaches* described in Tour 17.

Pensacola's location at the mouth of a deep water harbor has made it an important stronghold from the start of European exploration in the area. The city is highlighted in Tour 18.

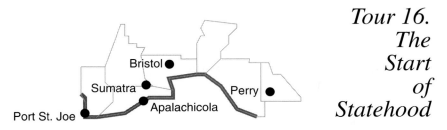

Tour 16. The Start of Statehood

The area combines vast stretches of timberland with several of Florida's important early communities. You will see a town which became a ghost town—and was then repopulated. You'll also see a replica of the first air conditioner invented and the site where Florida's first constitution was drafted.

Perry

The importance of forestry in Florida dates back to the early 1800s. The circular Visitor Center at the *Forest Capital State Cultural Museum* shows the development of the forestry industry in the area, with particular emphasis on the longleaf pine used to build so many of Florida's early homes.

Also on the property is the *North Florida Cracker Homestead Interpretive Site*. When settlers moved south from South Carolina, Virginia, and Georgia, they traveled in ox–drawn wagons, cracking their whips over the heads of their animals. For this reason, according to legend, they were called "Crackers." The house was built around 1863 and made with double–notched square logs. It is 60 feet long and has four rooms. They are a living room, a kitchen/dining room separated by a breezeway, called a dogtrot, and two bedrooms. The cedar shake shingles were made from cedar. The furnishings are of the period with simple chairs and tables. Also on the grounds are a vineyard, stable, hen house, general purpose shed, and an old turpentine still.

Location:	204 Forest Park Drive, South of Perry on US 19
Hours:	Thursday through Monday 9–12 and 1–5, closed Thanksgiving, Christmas, and New Year's Day
Fees:	Adults and children over 6 $1
Phone:	(904) 584–3227

Sumatra

During the War of 1812, the **Fort Gadsden State Historic Site** was used for recruiting and training Blacks and Indians. Its location served as a threat to supply vessels headed to the U.S. Territorial Boundary, 50 miles north. The British ordered the Fort's destruction. The battle which followed was one of the shortest in naval history. The fifth shot from the gunboats landed in the Fort's magazine killing 90% of the 300 men, women, and children sheltered there. A miniature replica of the original outpost and six historic exhibits are on display.

Location:	6 miles Southwest of Sumatra, off Route 65
Hours:	Daily 8–sunset
Fees:	No charge
Phone:	(904) 670–8616

Bristol

Some biblical historians say that Noah's Ark was built in **Torreya State Park**. They think the ark was built from lumber from the Torreya tree, which only grows in four locations in the world— Bristol, Northern California, Japan, and China. The scholars also note the location of the nearby rivers as being referenced in the **Bible**. Whether or not these issues can ever be resolved, **Torreya State Park** is an interesting place to see this unusual hardwood tree. We also enjoy walking to the steep riverside bluffs that rise more than 150 feet above the water. While visiting, make time to see the **Gregory House**, built in 1849 and moved to the park in 1935. It is furnished to reflect the lifestyles of the 1800s.

Location:	Home Carrier Route 2, 13 miles northwest of Bristol
Hours:	**Park**: Daily 8–sundown. **Tours**: Weekdays at 10, Weekends at 10, 2, and 4
Fees:	**Park**: $2 per vehicle. **Tours**: Adults $1, children over 13 50¢
Phone:	(904) 643–2674

Apalachicola

For 10,000 years, the Apalachee Indians occupied this land. Called the "land beyond the river," at least nine Spanish missions had been built in the area by 1665.

William Augustus Bowles, an Englishman, reached this section of the Gulf of Mexico in the 18th century. He was an adventurer and a pirate. Legend suggests that he came to Florida at the age of 12 and married the daughter of a Creek Indian Chief. He terrorized the Spaniards while trying to break their hold on East and West Florida. A somewhat different legend says that he was dismissed from the British Navy, moved to Georgia, mar-ried the Creek Indian woman, and became influential in tribal matters. In any event, he led a band of Creek against the Spanish in the Siege of Pensacola in 1781 and was taken prisoner by the Spaniards who imprisoned him in Madrid. In 1799, he escaped and rejoined the tribe near Apalachicola Bay. The Bay area became his headquarters and, for the next six years, he continued to loot surrounding towns and prey on ships at sea. He was again taken prisoner and died in 1805. Thus ended a frightening part of Apalachicola's history.

As cotton became an important agricultural crop in the Panhandle, Apalachicola harbor became famous. The town prospered. Imagine steamboats puffing their way into the harbor! However, as railroading matured, it signalled doom for the harbor area. Townspeople had to find another industry. By 1916, oysters began to be cultivated as a cash crop. The area now has more than 180,000 acres of oyster beds and sweet, delicious Apalachicola oysters are known throughout the world.

The *Apalachicola Historic District* includes most of the 1836 town plan with many 19th– and 20th–century buildings. Stroll down Fifth and Sixth Streets to see most of the pre–1860 buildings. Imagine cotton warehouses that stretched for three-quarters of a mile along the waterfront.

You probably arrived in Apalachicola in an air conditioned car. Try to imagine the city in 1845, before air conditioning was invented. A terrible yellow fever epidemic was spreading from house to house. The town's doctor, **John Gorrie,** was trying to ease his patients' suffering. In trying to make them more comfortable, he decided to cool the air and invented the first ice–making machine to provide air–cooled relief for his patients. Although Dr. Gorrie patented the invention in 1851, he had little cash. He was ridiculed in the national press and was unable to capitalize on the invention. He died in 1855 without having gained recognition for his work. Since that time, his original air conditioning machine has been placed on display in the Smithsonian Institution and a replica is part of the exhibit at the **John Gorrie State Museum**. It was the forerunner of modern refrigeration and air conditioning. The museum also shows other aspects of life in early Apalachicola.

Location:	6th Street at Avenue D
Hours:	Thursday through Monday 9–5. Closed Thanksgiving, Christmas and New Year's Day
Fees:	Adults and children over 6 $1
Phone:	(904) 653–9347

Port St. Joe

Although today's community is a growing timber and papermaking center with wide streets and lovely homes, it was not always so. In 1835, the village occupying the site was known as St. Joseph. For years, St. Joseph was a boom town competing with Apalachicola for the cotton and river trade.

Eighty–six territorial delegates met in 1838–39 at the site of today's **Constitution Convention State Museum**. They came to petition for statehood. Their task was to draft Florida's first constitution. St. Joseph became the meeting place only because it represented a neutral site between the political antagonists in Eastern/Western and Middle Florida.

Florida had been an American territory since 1821. Many Floridians, especially those living in the prosperous midsection, had long favored a change from territory to statehood status.

However, the powerful East and West Florida factions opposed statehood. Their argument was that Florida was too poor to assume the financial burdens statehood would impose. The first of Florida's five constitutions was drafted by the convention that met in St. Joseph on December 3, 1838. The political figures completed the framework for Florida's future on January 11, 1861.

On the same day the convention voted to submit the completed constitution to the people of the state for ratification, they also submitted paperwork to the U.S. Congress as the formal application on behalf of the people of Florida for admission to the Union. Talk about forgetting due process. For the next six years, the people of Florida spoke again and again about statehood. The beleaguered Legislative Council petitioned Congress for immediate admission to the Union, then for indefinite postponement, and then for division into two territories. Congress finally passed an act admitting Florida into the Union on March 3, 1845. As an important footnote, it should be noted that the state of Florida seceded from the Union in 1861, partially to avoid Civil War political and financial obligations, and rejoined the United States in 1865 after the Civil War had ended.

Location:	200 Allen Memorial Way
Hours:	Thursday through Monday 9–12 and 1–5, closed Thanksgiving, Christmas and New Year's Day
Fees:	Adults and children over 6 $1
Phone:	(904) 229–8029

It was mentioned that the town became a ghost town. During the boom it had grown to 12,000 inhabitants. In a short period of time, the city would be gone. First came a major yellow fever epidemic in 1841. Then came a hurricane in 1844. The survivors fled. Most of the abandoned houses and businesses were dismantled and moved by boat to Apalachicola. By 1846, all that remained of the village was the cemetery. The name change to Port St. Joe and the area's later settlement and growth have been largely due to the paper and pulp industry.

Bring a bucket and a rake. Wade into the bay and harvest a bucket of scallops! Check with the Chamber of Commerce for when scallops are in season and plan a special trip.

From sunrise...

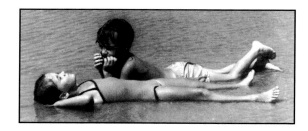

...to sunset,

*another perfect day on a
Florida beach.*

Tour 17.

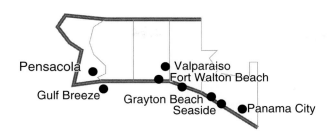

Extraordinary Beaches

By now, it is expected that the traveler anticipates surprises along the tour. Major military installations, past and present, provide a constant reminder of the area's importance in protecting the coastline and shipping lanes. Beachfront honky–tonk gives way to one of the country's most beautiful beaches near a modern–day rendition of a Florida seaside resort. Throughout the area, the tour combines Gulf Coast scenery with heavily wooded stretches.

Panama City

Spanish explorers landed here in the first half of the 16th-century. English settlement began about a hundred years later and American pioneers followed. *The Junior Museum of Bay County* tells the story of how the early pioneers lived, logged, and farmed. There are nature trails, a grist mill, and excellent science and nature hands-on exhibits for children.

Location:	1731 Jenks Avenue
Hours:	Monday through Friday 9–4:30, Saturday 10–4. Closed major holidays
Fees:	No charge, suggested donation $1
Phone:	(904) 769–6128 or 6129

Panama City Beach

The powdery, white sand beaches along this portion of the coast originated thousands of years ago as quartz crystals in the Appalachian Mountains. Over time, these crystals were sifted, washed, ground, polished, and slowly pushed south to be deposited along the beachfront. *City Pier* extends 1,600 feet into the Gulf of Mexico. Put a fishing line into the water. You very well may reel in tonight's dinner. Offshore, the *Yucatan Current*, part of the Gulf Stream, draws dolphin, marlin, sailfish, tuna, and other fish to the area. This is a fisherman's paradise.

The *Museum of Man in the Sea* is a wonderful place to climb through undersea vehicles. The museum has a collection of antique and military diving equipment and shows the history of underwater exploration. Try the hands-on experiments on diving bells and water pressure. There is also an excellent exhibit on the marine life in St. Andrew's Bay and a viewing pool.

Location:	17314 Panama City Beach Parkway
Hours:	Daily 9–5. Closed Thanksgiving, Christmas, and New Year's Day
Fees:	Adults $4, seniors over 65 $3.60, students and children 6–16 $2
Phone:	(904) 235–4101

Grayton Beach

Plan a visit to *Grayton Beach State Recreation Area.* You won't be disappointed! The park fronts on the Gulf of Mexico. It has beautiful clear water, gentle surf, and fine, white sand. Many experts consider this the most beautiful beach in the world—we agree! In addition to the gentle wave action of the Gulf of Mexico, nearby Western Lake is great for little children building sand castles and getting used to going to the beach. The lake also offers both salt and fresh water fishing.

Location:	Route 30A
Hours:	Daily 8-sunset
Fees:	$3.25 for day admission
Phone:	(904) 231-4210

Seaside

Seaside is an architectural gem which has won international acclaim. The beachside resort area is located along Route

30A and offers Victorian pitched roofs, white picket fences, and small town civilities. Robert Davis had inherited the land. He worked with Andres Duany and Elizabeth Plater–Zyberk, an architectural team, to create a new town that protected and respected the natural environment. The buildings incorporate the best of a number of Florida architectural styles. The building codes were so stringent that when adjoining communities and buildings were flattened by 1995's Hurricane Opal, Seaside weathered the storm with only marginal damage. The small community functions as a combination of residences, vacation homes, and rental cottages and suites and is set back from the beach. However, magnificent gazebos on the waterside frame the nightly Gulf of Mexico sunsets. Park in the shopping area, browse through the shops, and look carefully at the architecture and site usage. An architecture stop or a weekend visit is highly recommended.

> Location: Route 30A
> Phone: (904) 231–4224

Destin

In the 1830s, Captain Leonard A. Destin set sail from New England with three ships. Off this part of the Gulf Coast, they were caught in a hurricane. Two of the ships were wrecked and the third was beached. The survivors were attacked by Indians. The people who lived through both the hurricane and the attack decided to stay in the area that was then known as Choctawhatchee Bay, and was later named Destin.

The **De Soto Canyon** is located about 30 miles offshore and is a favorite spot for sailfishing.

Point Washington

William Henry Wesley founded a lumber company in the area. He also built 20 company–owned houses for workers and a company–owned store. His two story Greek Revival home is the centerpiece of the **Eden State Ornamental Gardens** site. The columned mansion was built in the late 1890s for his bride. It has a fireplace in each of the eight rooms. In typical 19th–century style, they are of equal size and arranged symmetrically on each floor. The house was built on piers to protect from flooding and to increase air circulation. It was built of native yellow pine. The furniture in the library is American Empire. There is also a 17th–century canopy bed in the Blue Room and a Victorian bed in the Red Room. Although the house is quite interesting, our favorite place to pause is in the gardens overlooking Choctawhatchee Bay.

Location:	North County Road 395, off US 98 between Panama City and Fort Walton Beach
Hours:	**Grounds:** Daily 8-sunset. **Mansion Tours:** Thursday through Monday 9–4, on the hour
Fees:	**Park:** $2 per vehicle or $1 for walkers or bikers. **Mansion:** Adults $1.50, children under 13 50¢
Phone:	(904) 231–4214

Fort Walton Beach

The area was once an important Indian settlement and meeting place. Over time, seven pre–Columbian cultures lived in the area. The *Indian Temple Mound Museum* tells the story of the Fort Walton Indian Culture's village which housed 1,000–2,000 people. In today's terminology, the settlement served as the "county seat" for the area's Indians. A large collection of woodland pottery has been found which dates back 3,500 years. A four-legged bowl is considered one of the most important ceramic artifacts existing in the Southeast. Exhibits in the museum show 10,000 years of Gulf Coast living by the Southern Indians.

Location:	139 Miracle Strip Parkway
Hours:	**September through May**: Monday through Saturday 11–4. **June through August:** Daily 9–5
Fees:	Adults $2.01, children 6–17 $1.01
Phone:	(904) 243–6521

Valpariso

Eglin is the largest air force base in the world. During World War II, a heroic group of pilots trained at *Eglin Air Force Base* for special duty with General James Doolittle.

The *Air Force Armament Museum* is the place to learn more about the Air Force. On the museum grounds, there is a fascinating display of planes, including the enormous F–105 Thunderchief (Vietnam era), the supersonic F–104 Starfighter, and a B–29 bomber. Of particular interest is the formerly top secret SR–71 Blackbird reconnaissance plane. This plane was so secret that its existence was denied for over 20 years. Inside the museum

C-141 Starlifter undergoes testing, 1964

there are over 5,000 items and interesting displays. We suggest beginning your visit with the film, *Arming the Air Force*. It screens continuously and tells the history of Eglin Air Force Base and its role in the development of armament. Also on the property is the *Eglin Air Force Base Climatic Laboratory.*

Location:	100 Museum Drive, Eglin Air Force Base
Hours:	Daily 9:30–4:30. Closed Thanksgiving, Christmas, and New Year's Day
Fees:	No charge
Phone:	(904) 882–4062

Gulf Breeze

Florida became a territory in 1821. Development of a fortification system along the coast began soon after. In both Florida and Mississippi, these forts are now part of the *Gulf Islands National Seashore* which also includes a 150 mile strip of barrier islands, natural harbors, and submerged lands stretching between Destin, Florida and Gulfport, Mississippi.

Florida's signature tree is the live oak. Its interesting history is shown at the *Naval Live Oaks Park*. The live oak has evergreen leaves, a leathery trunk, crooked branches, and can grow to 40–50 feet in height. It is often covered with Spanish moss and provides the shading canopies for so many of the older roads in the state. The area was originally developed as an experimental tree farm, a live oak plantation, for timber to build American ships. The Visitor Center includes exhibits on the history of the area. Take a self-guided nature walk through a stand of live oaks where the markers explain how the trees were selected As you begin to walk along the trails, notice the markers explaining how the trees were used in ship building.

In addition to its beauty, live oak timber has been important to the U.S. for over 200 years. The heaviest of all oak timber, it is resistant to disease and decay. Live oak timber from this area was used to build the *USS Constitution* in the 1790s. When the vessel was in action against the British during the War of 1812, it was nicknamed *Old Ironsides* because of the strength of its timber and its fine construction. In the 1930s, repairs were needed and, of course, live oak timber was used.

Location:	1801 Gulf Breeze Parkway
Hours:	**April through October**: Daily 8:30–5. **November through March**: Daily 9–4:30
Fees:	$4 per private vehicle with up to 8 people
Phone:	(904) 934–2600

Santa Rosa Island

Fort Pickens was built by the U.S. Corps of Engineers between 1829 and 1834 to assist in the defense of Pensacola Bay and the Naval Shipyard. Between 1886 and 1890 it was the prison for Geronimo, the Apache chief and medicine man. It is a good place for exploring. Also pause to look at the nature exhibits, the marine life aquariums, and to take a waterside tour.

Location:	1400 Fort Pickens Road
Hours:	**April through October:** Daily 8:30–5. **November through March:** , Daily 9-4:30 **Tours:** 11, 2 on weekends
Fees:	$4 per private vehicle with up to 8 people
Phone:	(904) 934–2600

Tour 18. Pensacola, City of Five Flags

Pensacola has one of the most colorful histories of any city in Florida. Although St. Augustine is recognized as the oldest continuous European settlement in the country, it should be noted that the *first* settlement was in Pensacola.

Spanish settlers arrived in Pensacola harbor in 1559. They stayed for two years before being driven away by hurricanes and Indian attacks. Soon after, the Spanish established another colony. However, hurricanes, a shortage of food, and a prevalence of disease caused te people in that settlement to perish. The Spaniards didn't return to Pensacola until about 100 years later. In 1693, a Spanish cartographer reported that he considered Pensacola Bay "the finest jewel possessed by his majesty."

From its settlement in 1559 to the Civil War, it changed hands 10 times and its residents lived under the flags of Spain, France, England, the Confederacy and the United States.

In the pre–Civil War period, Pensacola operated as a stockade, a frontier outpost, and a rollicking port city. Following the war, the timber industry prospered as pine and cypress forests were harvested.

Pensacola Harbor, early etching

Blue Angels, ca. 1962

No one knew how the community would support itself when the wood ran out. That occurred just as Pensacola became a military town. The establishment of the **U.S. Naval Air Station** in 1914 was the economic turning point. Today, the Pensacola **Naval Air Station** is one of the country's major military facilities. Try to plan a visit when a Winging Ceremony is taking place. It often concludes with a Blue Angels Airshow.

The **National Museum of Naval Aviation** is a national treasure. The museum covers 250,000 square feet and is over three stories tall, with a seven–story, glass and steel atrium featuring four Blue Angel Skyhawks suspended from the ceiling in a diamond formation. This is one of the three largest air and space museums in the world. If it is manmade and flies, look for it here first!

To highlight just a few items in the collection, we suggest the following. The west wing is devoted to World War II carrier aviation. There is a reproduction of a World War II Pacific Theater flight deck, complete with carrier island, signal flags, and gun tubs. In another part of the museum, directly across from the F–4U Corsairs and F–6F Hellcats is their arch rival plane, the Mitsubishi A–6M2B Zero. There are over 100 aircraft, an exact replica of an Apollo Space Suit, a Lunar Rover Vehicle, and almost 100 scale models of aircraft, dirigibles, and spacecraft. It's fun to try the F–

4 and A–7 jet cockpit simulators. Strap yourself in and take the controls! We also enjoy looking at the NC–4 Flying Boat. In 1919 it became the first plane to cross the Atlantic Ocean. If you have children with you, don't miss the Flight Adventure Deck.

Location:	3465 Taylor Road, on the Naval Air Station
Hours:	Daily 9–5, closed Thanksgiving, Christmas, and New Year's Day
Fees:	No charge
Phone:	(904) 452–3604

Long before the Naval Air Station was established, two forts were built in the early 19th century to protect the emerging Pensacola Navy Yard. *Fort San Carlos de Barrancas* was built between 1839–1844. It was only manned by soldiers during the Civil War. The *Advanced Redoubt* was built a little later. It also was only manned by soldiers during the Civil War. Be sure to stop at the Information Center before walking through the Fort.

Location:	Southeast of Navy Boulevard, on the Naval Air Station
Hours:	**April to October:** 9:30–5. **November to March:** Daily 10:30–4. **Tours: June and July**: Daily 11–2. **August through May**: Sunday at 2. Closed Christmas
Fees:	No charge
Phone:	(904) 452–2311

A good place to learn about Pensacola's past is *Historic Pensacola Village.* It presents nine restorations of colonial Pensacola buildings dating from 1803. The complex provides a chance to look at West Florida's history through the *Museum of Commerce,* the *Museum of Industry,* the *Julee Cottage Museum of Black History,* the *Dorr, Lavalle and Quina House Museums* and several others. Within this small district, it is possible to see examples of how early residents lived, as well as beautiful examples of Spanish, French Creole, and Greek Revival architecture.

The *T. T. Wentworth, Jr. Florida State Museum* is housed in what used to be the City Hall. It is a large Renaissance Revival–style building built in 1907–08. The collection tells the almost unbroken history of Pensacola and West Florida, from the earliest settlement attempts by the Spanish to the development of today's city.

Location:	**Historic Village:** 205 East Zaragoza Street
	Wentworth Museum: 320 Jefferson Street
Hours:	Monday through Saturday 10–4. **House Tours:**
	11:30, 1:30, 2:30. Closed all state holidays
Fees:	One ticket admits guests to both the Village and the
	Wentworth Museum. Adults $6, seniors over 65,
	active military, and students $5, children 4–16 $2.50
Phone:	(904) 444–8905

When you're ready to walk into the 20th–century, go to the *North Hill Preservation District*. The 50 block area is roughly boundaried by LaRua, Palafox, Blount, and Reus Streets. It contains over 500 homes, many of which were built in the city's lumbering era. This is one of the loveliest residential and historic districts in the state.

During the American Revolutionary War, the Spanish government helped colonists work to win their independence from England. Secretly, the Spaniards sent money, guns, medical supplies, and food from Havana, Cuba. By 1779, the Spanish governor of Louisiana was responsible for removing the British from the Gulf of Mexico. By 1781, he had 7,000 soldiers from Cuba. At that time, Pensacola was the most important British stronghold on the Gulf Coast. After a two month battle, the British surrendered at what is now *Fort George*. Follow the markers in the park to learn more about the battle.

Location:	Palafox and La Rua Streets

Pensacola's oldest settlement began in what is now the *Seville Historic District,* an area surrounding 130 East Government Street. This section of town has been particularly important since the late 1700s and now has a rare concentration of Creole, Victorian, and other homes dating from the 1780s to the late 1800s.

An elaborate boardwalk and nature trail network and an observation tower at East Beach provide bird watchers with excellent views overlooking the marsh. Plan to be at *Big Lagoon State Recreation Area* at sunset to watch the great blue heron stalk its dinner or settle in for the night. The park also includes beaches, two swimming areas on Big Lagoon, and a passageway to the Intracoastal Waterway.

Location: 12301 Gulf Beach Highway
Hours: Daily 8-sunset
Fees: $3.25 per vehicle with up to 8 people
Phone: (904) 492–1595

Great Blue Herons

The
Northern
Panhandle

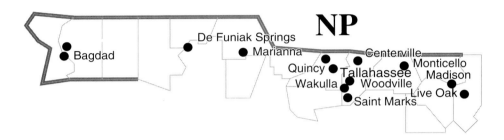

The Northern Panhandle is, ironically, the most "Southern" part of Florida you will visit. Four tours are highlighted in this section.

In Tour 19, we travel along *The Spanish Explorers Trail* to find springs and towns which are relatively untouched by the 20th-century.

Tallahassee, The Capitol Connection leads to the two capitol buildings in the heart of the city. After taking a good look at government in action, make time for museums, universities, scenery, and history. They are all part of Tour 20.

Indian myths and pioneers populate Tour 21 as you explore *Canopy Roads and Indian Springs.*

The last tour in this section, *The Tobacco Road*, returns to the days of plantations and tobacco auctions as you continue to put today's Florida into perspective.

Tour 19.
The
Spanish
Explorers
Trail

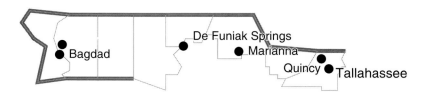

Many Spanish explorers traveled north from Pensacola along old Indian trails. They mapped the trails and the route then became known as the Old Spanish Trail. Although Ponce de León was one of the most famous 16th-century explorers to travel this way, realize that many Indians, explorers, settlers, and modern day transportation specialists have all had a part in developing this route. Highlights of the trip include seeing part of the antebellum South and noting agricultural communities which once made this region prosperous.

Bagdad

What imagination someone had as they were naming the town—and what a wonderful name to find in lumbering country! As had been the case with Pensacola, Bagdad's lumbering economy flourished from around 1820 to 1930. Today, its economic prosperity has passed, leaving behind a quiet village with dozens of restored Victorian houses.

Milton

Once Milton was a thriving outpost of sawmills, lumbermen, and townspeople. Four–masted schooners and shipping steamers landed at its piers. Today's community is much more quiet. The *Milton Opera House* and *Imogene Theatre* in the center of town have been restored and remind us of the city's early cultural legacy.

A quick trip into the 20th-century awaits you with a visit to *Whiting Field*, the busiest military airport in the Southeast and the most efficient military airport in the world for training. It is the center for the military's T–34 fixed wing aircraft and TH–57 helicopter training. Tours are available with advance reservation and are quite interesting—particularly if you've always wanted to crawl into a T–34 and see a flight simulator. There are vintage aircraft on display as well as the planes currently in use.

Location:	8 miles north of Milton on Highway 87
Hours:	**Tours**: Phone ahead and make tour arrangements well in advance. For those with advance reservations only, tours are given Monday through Friday 7:30–2
Fees:	No charge
Phone:	(904) 623–7651

Holt

General Andrew Jackson walked an Indian trading trail through part of the Florida Territory in 1818. In *Blackwater River State Park* you can hike the same route, now known as the Jackson Red Ground Hiking Trail. Follow the red paint markings from Karick Lake to the Red Rock Picnic Area over a combination of footpaths and forest roadways. The Jackson Trail is part of the National Recreation Trail System and the Florida Trail System.

Location:	Off US 90, 15 miles northeast of Milton
Hours:	Daily, 8-sunset
Fees:	$3.25 per vehicle for up to eight people
Phone:	(904) 983-5363

DeFuniak Springs

In the early 20th-century, this small town became one of Florida's leading intellectual centers. It was the site of a winter Chautauqua camp. Turn off the highway and take a pleasant drive around the circular spring–fed lake. While driving, note the white

Chautauqua buildings on the western side of the lake and stop at the small library to see their amazing collection of armor. Some items in the collection date back to the Crusades.

Marianna

Founded in 1829, Marianna was named for the daughters of a pioneer merchant. The town grew because of its location as a covered wagon crossing point and as one of the stops on the stage coach route.

Stop at the *Florida Caverns State Park* to cool off on a hot day. There are wonderful local legends about the limestone caverns ranging from how people were hidden in them to how some of the important townspeople came and went between the caverns and city buildings. Today's visit to the caves is a cool treat. Be sure to bring a sweater with you to wear once you go underground. The 50 mile Chipola River Canoe Trail, part of the Florida Canoe Trail System, begins here.

Location:	3 miles north on Route 167
Hours:	**Park**: Daily 8–sunset. **Cave tour**: Daily 9–4. The tours are popular and sometimes sell out. Plan to get your ticket as soon as you arrive at the park.
Fees:	**Park:** $3.25 per private vehicle up to 8 people, $1 for hikers or bikers. **Cave tour**: Adults $4, children 3–12 $2.
Phone:	(904) 482–9598

...gone Canoeing

Quincy

Settled around 1824, Quincy attracted wealthy planters and politicians from the North. There was a great deal of sentiment against the Union forces throughout this part of Florida and Quincy's citizens were among the most belligerent, anti–Unionists in the State. A few years before Florida seceded from the Republic, Quincy Guards seized arms and ammunition from a U.S. Arsenal on the Apalachicola River.

In 1893, a deposit of Fullers earth was discovered along the riverbanks in the area. The clay was open–pit mined in a 25mile radius of the town. By the 1930s, the area produced more than half the Fullers earth used in the U.S.

The land, its natural resources, and quick thinking helped Quincy residents become millionaires. Early in the 20th century, Mark W. "Pat" Monroe was a Quincy banker. He heard about Coca–Cola from friends in Georgia. He urged his neighbors and the bank's customers to buy stock in the company—the bank even lent them money to do so. At one time, over 65% of all Coca-Cola stock was owned by Quincy residents and many fortunes were made. So, the next time you're in Quincy, open a Coke and think about how one man's belief in a stock caused economic prosperity for a town.

As you stroll through the community, note the old fashioned gardens of jasmine and camellias, as well as the beautiful Queen Anne and Greek Revival homes in the 36-block historic district.

Tour 20.
Tallahassee,
The
Capitol
Connection

Tallahassee

Tallahassee is Florida's capitol city and owes that honor to its location. At the time of statehood, peninsular Florida had not been widely settled and had not emerged as a political force. The state's major political figures were from Pensacola and Jacksonville. These factions rarely agreed on anything and were competitive in almost everything. It was clear that neither group would give in and let the other city be chosen as the new state capitol. Tallahassee was selected simply because it was located midway between the home cities of the political rivals.

Florida's legislation is enacted in the **State Capitol**, also known as the **New Capitol**. Call ahead to check the Spring legislative schedule and then watch government in action. If no sessions are underway, go to the 22nd floor observatory for a panoramic view of the city. This building, opened in 1977, was one of the last designed by Edward Durrell Stone.

Location:	South Adams Street
Hours:	**Building:** Monday through Friday 9–12 and 1–3. Self-guided tour information at the Visitor Information Center on the Plaza level
Fees:	No charge
Phone:	(904) 488–6167

It is rare to find a state with two capitol buildings. The *Old Capitol* has been restored to its 1902 appearance and is a good starting point to review the state's historic displays. Of particular interest is the permanent exhibit which tells the story of Florida's colorful and vibrant political history.

Location:	400 South Monroe Street at Apalachee Parkway
Hours:	Monday through Friday 9–4:30, Saturday 10–4:30, Sunday and holidays 12–4:30. Closed Christmas
Fees:	No charge
Phone:	(904) 487–1902

The *Florida Vietnam Era Veterans' Memorial* frames the Old Capitol. It was designed by James Kolb, a Sarasota artist. With over 1,900 names inscribed, this is a moving reminder of the contribution those brave Floridians made for their country.

Location:	State Capitol Complex
Hours:	Daily, 24 hours
Fees:	No charge
Phone:	(904) 487–1533

Search for the sunken treasures of old Spanish galleons, examine Civil War memorabilia, and learn more about the steamboat era at the *Museum of Florida History*. And these exhibits are only the beginning when you visit this major state resource.

Location:	500 South Bronough Street, lower level of the R. A. Gray Building
Hours:	Monday through Friday 9–4:30, Saturday 10–4:30, Sunday and holidays 12–4:30. Closed Thanksgiving and Christmas
Fees:	No charge, donations welcome
Phone:	(904) 488–1484

Two interesting areas for a walk or a drive are the *Calhoun Street Historical District Downtown* and the *Park Avenue Historical District Downtown*. Much of the housing stock was built in the 1830–1880 period and has been restored.

In 1856, Peres Bonney Brokaw began building his Italianate, two–story mansion. Now known as the *Brokaw–McDougall House and Gardens*, it houses the Tallahassee Preservation Board. Ask for an informational brochure and take a self-guided tour of this interesting building.

Location:	329 North Meridian
Hours:	Monday through Friday 8–5
Fees:	No charge
Phone:	(904) 488–3901

The next portion of the tour involves short drives beyond the downtown district.

Enjoy the *Tallahassee Museum of History and Natural Science* and safely see a Florida panther's habitat and a red wolf's den. Although there are many wonderful exhibits, children especially like the Discovery Center and the Zoo.

Children of all ages enjoy visiting Big Bend Farm, a recreated 19th–century farm. The word Big Bend refers to the big bend of the Florida Gulf Coast. The three family farms built in the 1880s and 1890s were moved from that area. Throughout the year, museum interpreters demonstrate the skills a farm family needed to survive in Florida of the 1880s.

Bellevue is on the grounds of the museum. It is a one and a half story frame home, once owned by Princess Catherine Murat who lived there from 1854 to 1867. She was the grandniece of George Washington and the widow of Prince Achille Murat, the exiled Prince of Naples and nephew of Napoleon Bonaparte. Although the house is humble, she named it Bellevue, French for lovely vista. It originally sat on 520 acres of land and was moved to its present location in 1967. The interior has been restored to the period when the princess lived there.

Location:	3945 Museum Drive
Hours:	Monday through Saturday 9–5, Sunday 12:30–5, closed major holidays
Fees:	Adults $6, seniors over 62 $5.50, children 4–15 $4.
Phone:	(904) 575–8684 or 576–1636

In 1923, the *Alfred B. Maclay State Gardens* property was purchased. The 3,386-square-foot cypress house had been built around 1909 as a hunting lodge. Mr. Maclay, a New York financier, and his wife Louise renovated the house. Mrs. Maclay was largely responsible for creating the 28 acre ornamental garden as

part of their winter retreat. One rare feature of the house is its birdseye cypress paneled library. The library floor is made of 18–inch–wide long leaf yellow pine cut and milled on the property. The best time to visit is January through April when most of the camellias and azaleas are in full bloom. There are about 150 varieties of camellias and about 50 varieties of azaleas. Take a few moments to find the walled garden—and then lose yourself in its serenity. Make time to enjoy the picnic pavilion and then hike the Big Pine Nature Trail that meanders through the wooded hillside overlooking Lake Hall.

Location:	3540 Thomasville Road
Hours:	**Park and Gardens:** Daily 8–sunset. **House:** January through early April: Daily 9–5. **House Tours in March:** Saturdays and Sundays (call ahead for dates and times)
Fees:	**Park and Gardens:** $3.25 per vehicle, including up to 8 people. $1 for hikers and bikers. **House Tour:** Adults $3, children 6–12 $1.50
Phone:	(904) 487–4556

B*eadel House* is a two–story frame house built in 1895 in the Vernacular Colonial Revival–style. The land was originally a cotton plantation. Later, it became a lodge for wealthy Northerners who came to hunt quail. The original section of the house was built around 1895 by Edward Beadel, a New York architect. His nephew, Henry, a noted photographer, left the estate to be used as an ecological research station—*Tall Timbers*—which is mainly known for quail research. The living room and study contain books, photographic equipment, and tools used for research and collecting by Henry Beadel. The library is paneled in brown sweet gum wood with heavy oak beams supporting its 12 foot high ceiling. The house faces Lake Iamonia and is screened by live oaks and magnolias. It is interesting for both its contemporary use and for its history.

Location:	Route 1, County Road 12
Hours:	**Tours**: Second Sunday of the month 2:15 and 3:15
Fees:	No charge
Phone:	(904) 893–4153

A lthough the *Lake Jackson Indian Mounds State Archaeological Site* is a now a quiet park, it was once one of the most important gathering places for Indians of this region. It was the site of an Indian village and trading center. There are two earthen pyramid shaped burial mounds on the site. They are thought to be part of the remains of a ceremonial center that existed between 1300 and 1600 AD. The largest mound is 278 feet by 312 feet at the base and approximately 36 feet in height. It can be climbed by using the boardwalk. The Indians who lived here were farmers who traded their surplus crops with nearby villages. While in the park, find your way to the lake. It is said that Hernando De Soto and his army spent the winter of 1539 living in the Indian village. It was here that the first Christmas celebration in the New World was held.

Location:	3600 Indian Mounds Road
Hours:	Daily 8–sunset
Fees:	No charge
Phone:	(904) 562–0042 or 922–6007

S*an Luis Archaeological and Historic Site* was the location of a Spanish town, founded in 1633. In the late 1500s and early

1600s, Spain established a chain of missions across Florida. By the mid–1600s, San Luis de Talimali was the center of the mission system. There was a fort, a church complex, and an Apalachee Indian council house and village. Many of the Mission's supplies were shipped from Havana, Cuba through the port of St. Marks on the Gulf Coast. When Britain invaded the area in 1704, residents decided their town would not be captured. They burned it to the ground.

Visitors are welcome to watch state archaeologists at the 50 acre site as more of this important historic village is uncovered. Take the trail walk to see exhibits that tell the story of the early inhabitants, as well as today's search for the past. Also try to make time to see the Indian and Spanish artifacts and plan to take a guided tour.

Location:	2020 Mission Road
Hours:	Monday through Friday 9–4:30, Saturday 10–4:30, Sunday 12–4:30. Closed Thanksgiving and Christmas. **Excavations and Tours**: Call ahead for schedule
Fees:	No charge
Phone:	(904) 487–3711

...gone fishing, ca. 1910.
Although you won't find these fish, try your luck at Lake Jackson

Centerville
Wakulla Woodville
Saint Marks

Tour 21.
Canopy
Roads
and
Indian
Springs

Tour 21 is for people who take their leisure seriously. If you have time before leaving Tallahassee, stop at the State Archives and search out some of the early maps. The old Canopy Roads, planted by Florida's pioneers are perfect for a leisurely afternoon outing. Bring a bathing suit and look for legendary creatures, bike the old railroad route, and just relax.

Heading North

Canopy Roads are Florida's moss–draped, live oak boundaried by-ways. They serve as a reminder of stage coach days and the era when early settlers came in creaking wagon trains along dirt roads seeking their new Florida homesteads. The early settlers planted their roadways with live oak trees. Now secondary roads, five of the state's old canopied settlers' routes are particularly beautiful. The old Centerville Road is featured in this tour. When you have time, also plan to find the Meridian, Miccosukee, Old Bainbridge, and St. Augustine canopy roads. They are all noted for their beauty.

Heading South

The Tallahassee–St. Marks Railroad was Florida's oldest continuously operating railroad. It was the first railroad under construction in Florida and the first railroad in the nation to receive a Federal land grant. The 20 mile line moved cotton and other products from the Northern Panhandle to the port of St. Marks from 1837–1884. For its first 12 years, mules hauled freight and passenger cars along the roadbed. By the 1850s, engines were used. The line was in service for 147 years.

Florida's first designated state trail, the ***Tallahassee–St. Marks Railroad Trail***, follows the abandoned rail bed of the historic railroad for 16 miles. The eight foot wide corridor was preserved as a recreational trail for walking, hiking, and biking. It is one of the safest bike trails in the state and is particularly enjoyable because it ends near the ***Marcos de Apalachee State Historic Site*** in St. Marks. Access to the trail is at the paved parking

lot on State Road 363 just south of State Road 261 near Tallahassee, or the parking lot adjacent to the ***Marcos de Apalachee State Historic Site*** in St. Marks.

Tallahassee bike riders enjoy an outing

Woodville

From March 1–3, 1865, during the final weeks of the Civil War, a Union flotilla assembled in Apalachee Bay. The troops planned to march north, destroy Confederate supplies, and take Tallahassee. Since the Panhandle was largely Confederate territory, the Tallahassee Confederates received an early warning of the planned attack. Early on the morning of March 6, 1865, Confederate volunteers and Union forces met at what is now the ***Natural Bridge Battlefield Historic Site***. Before the day was over, the Union forces were defeated. The Battle at Natural Bridge kept Union troops from reaching Tallahassee and, in that way, may have kept the city from falling to Union troops.

Location:	Natural Bridge Road, 6 miles East of Woodville
Hours:	Daily 8–sunset
Fees:	No charge
Phone:	(904) 922–6007

Wakulla Springs

Old Indian legends tell of tiny water people who lived in Wakulla Springs, which they named Mysteries of Strange Water. They were four inches tall and had long hair. On moonlit nights, they danced in the depths of the Springs. At a certain hour, late at night, a mysterious warrior appeared in a stone canoe and frightened them away. Come to the Springs and see what you find!

Edward Ball Wakulla Springs State Park is the site of the state's deepest freshwater springs, explored to a depth of 250 feet. The water is so clear that objects at the deepest point of the Springs are clearly visible. In fact, in the 1800s, people in rowboats used glass–bottomed buckets to look into the water. The rate of flow is about 10,000 gallons per second and the basin covers four and a half acres. The river it spawns runs 16 miles to the Gulf of Mexico. Because of the pristine setting, numerous Hollywood productions were filmed here, including some of the early Tarzan movies and *Creature from the Black Lagoon.*

Edward Ball, a conservationist, financier, member of the duPont family, and political figure bought the property. In 1937, he built a 27 room, Spanish–style lodge, now the heart of the property. It is a fine place for a meal or an overnight stay. Particularly note the Tennessee marble floors, the blue heron fireplace andirons, the lobby ceiling, and the rafters with their handpainted Toltec and Aztec designs. Come for a swim, a glass–bottomed boat ride, a trail hike, or a jungle boat cruise down the river. All are fine ways to view waterlife, wildlife, lush vegetation, and to consider whether that evening shadow was really one of the legendary water people.

Location:	Wakulla Springs Road, Route 61, 13 miles South of Tallahassee
Hours:	**Park:** Daily 8–sunset. **Glass Bottom Boat Cruises:** Daily 11–3, when the water is clear. **River Cruises:** Daily 9:45–5. Hours may vary in the winter.
Fees:	**Park:** $3.25 per vehicle. **Boat Tours**: Adult $4.50, children under 13 $2.25
Phone:	(904) 922–3632

St. Marks

The remains of a Spanish fort and mission are located at the *San Marcos de Apalachee State Historic Site and Museum*. The area was first occupied by Spanish in 1528 as they walked overland from the area that is now near Tampa. In 1679, they built their first fort which was burned down by pirates in 1682. About 35 years later, the Spanish built a second wooden fort and, in 1739, they started a stone fort. The history of the area is long and colorful with Creek Indians, Spanish, British, Confederates, and Union troops all occupying the site at different times. Of particular interest is the fact that a Union hospital was built here in 1857 to treat ill sailors. A lovely trail winds through the Confederate earthenworks, climbs to the top of a powder magazine, follows the protected fort walls along the banks of the Wakulla River, and ends at the original site of early Spanish fortifications where the Wakulla and St. Mark's Rivers merge.

Location:	148 Old Fort Road, one mile southwest of Rt. 363
Hours:	Thursday through Monday 9–5, closed Thanksgiving, Christmas, and New Year's Day
Fees:	Adults and children over 6 $1
Phone:	(904) 922–6007

In 1521, the Spanish established one of the first shipbuilding yards in what is now *St. Mark's National Wildlife Refuge*. The 70,000 acre area has a diverse collection of wildlife. It also houses the 1831 St. Mark's Lighthouse. Its scenic hiking trail is part of the Florida Trail.

Location:	Off County Road 59, 3 miles south of Newport
Hours:	**Refuge:** Daily sunrise–sunset. **Visitor Center:** Monday through Friday 8–4:15. Saturday and Sunday 10–5
Fees:	$4 per private vehicle with up to 8 people, $1 for hikers and bikers
Phone:	(904) 925–6121

Tour 22.
The
Tobacco
Road

The strong economic and political roots of this part of the state developed from the Civil War era. Confederate plantation owners came south to expand their holdings. The tour winds through small Southern towns whose antebellum architecture combines with history to provide an unusual tour.

Monticello

The town was founded by planters from Georgia and the Carolinas in the early 1800s. They built magnificent homes and planted the **Avenue of Oaks** in 1889. It is one of the main approaches to Monticello and provides a historic frame to the architecture, the landscaping, and the sense of an earlier Florida.

Madison

Transplanted Sea Island cotton growers from South Carolina settled the town in 1838. First they planted, then they installed the world's largest long staple cotton gin. Cotton became the cash crop core of the community. In 1916 when there was a major boll weevil infestation, the

Dixie Plantation House,
Jefferson County

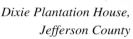

economy was almost ruined. The rebuilding has been slow and many signs of the earlier times remain. Although Confederate sympathies were strong throughout the northern portion of the state, Madison and Monticello were particularly vocal in their views. When Florida seceded from the Union the townspeople were so pleased that they rang bells, built a bonfire, and had a party.

Confederate Square is at the heart of the community. The square was once the site of a blockhouse used as a refuge for women and children during the Seminole Indian War and was also a gathering place for sympathizers during the Civil War. Stop to read the plaques and tablets, and look at the monuments. If you're lucky, there might be a program scheduled at the bandstand. Walk, browse, and drive slowly through this town to explore some of the residential area, the courthouse, and the shopping district.

Live Oak

The live oak came first, the town's name followed. There once was an old wagon road that ran from a military post at Suwannee Springs to the Gulf of Mexico. It passed a clear, deep pond under a huge live oak. Since the setting offered shade and a pretty camping ground, the area became known as Live Oak. When the railroad came through, the name became official.

For centuries parts of the Northern Panhandle have been known as tobacco growing regions. Tobacco was grown and smoked by Indians long before the appearance of European explorers. The first record of its use in the state appeared in a 1564 entry in the log of Captain John Hawkins, a pirate.

In the 1890s, shade tobacco was introduced in the area. For many years, in order to sell their tobacco, Florida growers transported their leaf to auctions farther north. Live Oak business people established a tobacco auction in their town to avoid the long trip to North Carolina. As you drive into town, imagine that it is the first week in August early in the 20th–century. The roads, of course, are unpaved. The hot Florida summer sun shines through a hazy filter of dirt and dust. It is hot. People are everywhere. For weeks before the auction, farmers and their families—with wagons loaded with tobacco leaf—have been arriving from all directions.

There is a sense of anticipation. Owners take their burlap bags of tobacco into a warehouse where it is examined, weighed, and the bags are stacked in rows on the floor. Each stack is given a lot number, ticketed with the owner's name, and the total lot's weight is recorded. The owners then sit near their tobacco. An auctioneer, surrounded by a cloud of buyers and observers, walks up and down the rows. The group stops before each lot and the bidding begins. The noise level rises as heated bidding occurs. If the owner is dissatisfied with the bid, the walking auction will pass by, leaving the owner to wait for the next day's auction to try for a better price. When the auctioneer yells "SOLD," the buyer has the burlap bags rapidly moved to nearby wagons, trucks, or railroad cars; the auction crew clears the space, the next sellers bring their tobacco into the warehouse, and the process starts again.

And that's how it was at a tobacco auction in Live Oak.

Tobacco was grown under slats, ca. 1910

North
Central
Florida

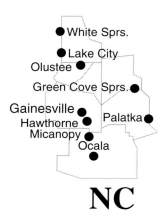

NC

Although composer Stephen Foster had never seen the state or the river, his melodies and memories form the core of the **Suwannee River** Tour.

The **Thoroughbreds All** tour begins deep in steamboat country and continues to Ocala, an area noted for its thoroughbred horses, to Gainesville and its university and to Hawthorne to visit the home of Marjorie Kinnan Rawlings, author of **The Yearling**.

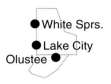
● White Sprs.
● Lake City
Olustee ●

Tour 23.
A Composer
and the
Suwannee
River

White Springs

Seminole and Timucuan Indians considered White Springs a sacred area. They marked trees in a five–mile circle around the sulphur springs. Warriors wounded in battle would not be attacked as long as they recuperated within the boundaried area.

A white settlement was founded in 1826 on the north bank of the Suwannee River. By the turn of the century, the village of White Springs was known as a health resort. It attracted many Northern tourists.

Around the time of the Civil War, the area became known as Rebels Refuge. Georgia and Carolina plantation owners moved here to wait out the war in relative safety, out of the path of the Union invasion.

The *Stephen Foster State Folk Culture Center* is located on the banks of the Suwannee River. It honors the memory of American composer Stephen C. Foster who was born near Pittsburgh, Pennsylvania on July 4, 1826. One of America's best known musical storytellers, he wrote the song now known as *S'wanee River* in 1851 and sold it to famed minstrelman E. P. Christy. Mr. Foster went on to author about 200 songs during his prolific career.

It is tragic to realize that Stephen Foster, a man who brought so much music to the world, died alone in New York City. At his death, he was almost penniless.

While discussing his music, a moment must be taken to comment that Stephen Foster never, ever saw the Suwannee River. When he finished composing *Old Folks at Home,* as the song was originally known, Stephen Foster was in Pittsburgh. He asked his brother for help. When the song was written, he had named it for the Pee Dee River in South Carolina. But he wanted a more musical sounding name. His brother pulled down an atlas. After the names of several Southern rivers had been rejected, he looked at Florida's map. What about the Suwannee River (or as they spelled it, the S'wanee)? Perfect! And so the song was named.

The *Stephen Foster State Folk Cultural Center* combines a carillon, Stephen Foster exhibits, and displays of Florida folklife. It is easy to imagine the days when the steamboats were traveling along the St. Johns River and Stephen Foster's tunes were being sung by the minstrels. In addition to wonderful exhibits, this is a peaceful spot to take a quiet walk along one of the trails leading to the river or the Center. Listen to the Westminster chimes which sound on the quarter hour and arrange your schedule so that you can listen to Stephen Foster's melodies which are played four times

daily. Before leaving, stop to gaze at flowing the Suwannee River, listen to the bells, perhaps hum a line from a Stephen Foster melody, and thank the composer for his contribution to America's music.

Stephen Foster Mural in the State Folk Cultural Center

Location:	White Springs, off US 41 North
Hours:	**Park**: Daily 8–sunset. **Buildings**: Daily 9–5
Fees:	$3.25 per car, including up to 8 people per vehicle, $1 for hikers and bikers
Phone:	(904) 397-4331

Lake City

Florida's *Sports Hall of Fame* highlights the accomplishments of more than 100 nationally known athletes, coaches, and sports personalities. It is a perfect place to remember some of the great moments in American sports history.

Location:	601 Hall of Fame Drive
Hours:	Daily 9-5, Sunday 10-4
Fees:	Adults and children over 12 $6
Phone:	(904) 758–1310

Olustee

The largest Civil War conflict in Florida was fought at what is now the *Olustee Battlefield State Historic Site*. On February 20, 1864, twelve regiments of Union troops engaged 5,000 Confederate soldiers. The story of the defeat of the Union troops is told in the museum on the grounds and the large monument is dedicated to those who fought and died here. Each February, a reenactment of the battle is held. Phone ahead for details.

Location:	2–1/2 miles east of Olustee on US 90
Hours:	Thursday through Monday 9–5
Fees:	No charge, donations welcome
Phone:	(904) 758-0400

...gone hiking,

Ocala National Forest

Green Cove Springs

In the late 1870s and 1880s, Green Cove Springs was a fashionable winter resort. Steamboats from as far away as Charleston and Savannah travelled the St. Johns River and landed passengers at the resort piers. President Grover Cleveland and well–to–do Northerners came annually. Gail Borden, condensed milk manufacturer, and J.C. Penney, chain store magnate, bought property here and took active roles in the development of the town. About eight miles away, at Penney Farms, Mr. Penney built the ***Penney Farms Memorial Community*** to honor his parents. There are 96 apartments and a chapel. Dedicated in 1927, this is a home for retired religious leaders of all denominations.

While in Green Cove Springs, drive past ***St. Mary's Church*** which was built in 1878. It is one of the best examples of Carpenter Gothic architecture in the state and is located on St. John's Avenue.

Palatka

Palatka developed as an early trading and lumbering town. During the Civil War, it was occupied by Union troops. After the war, like Green Cove Springs, it became a fashionable winter resort. Easterners would travel by train to Jacksonville and then take the steamboat to town. In its heyday, there were nine resort hotels, including the Putnam House with 400 rooms. Palatka was also a political center where many of the prominent Florida politicians of the era lived or visited.

Bronson–Mulholland House is a three story cypress plantation–style home with Greek Revival lines. It was built in 1854 for Judge Isaac Bronson, one of Florida's major political figures and one of the state's first circuit riders. ***Putnam Historic Museum***, located nearby, is housed in the oldest building in Putnam County. Its exhibits are reminiscent of the county in the early days after the Civil War.

Location:	100 Madison Street at First Street
Hours:	Tuesday, Thursday, and Sunday, 2–5
Fees:	No charge, donations welcome
Phone:	(904) 329–0140

During the 1930s, one of the area's WPA projects was the planting of over 70,000 camellias and azaleas and thousands of subtropical trees and shrubs at the ***Ravine State Gardens***. Today's displays are magnificent, particularly in February and March. Be careful as you cross one of the two Swinging Bridges across the ravine. Once you, or your teenager, start the bridge swinging, it will continue to give you a frightening walk until you reach the other side. The Court Estates, another WPA project, is composed of 50 columns of limestone from which all of the U.S. State flags are flown on public holidays. We enjoy taking the two mile, one way driving tour that circles the ravine before starting a hike.

Location:	1600 Twigg Street
Hours:	Daily, 8–sunset. Road closes to traffic at 4 pm
Fees:	$3.25 per car, including up to 8 people per vehicle or $1 for hikers or bikers
Phone:	(904) 329–3721

Dating from the early 1850s, ***St. Mark's Episcopal Church*** was designed by Richard Upjohn, architect of New York's Trinity Church. During the Civil War, Union troops used it as their shelter. Although it is not open to the public, it is an interesting example of church building of the period and is located at 200 Main Street.

Gainesville

It is hard to look around today's Gainesville and realize that residents once graced it with the name of Hog Town. As the community grew, they realized the name was no longer appropriate and renamed the town to honor General Edmund Gaines, who had captured Aaron Burr and was the victorious commander of the Second Seminole War.

Bring the kids and plan to spend an afternoon at one of the top natural history museums in the country. The *Florida Museum of Natural History* is an outstanding resource. We particularly enjoy the scale model of the Mayan Temple, 790 AD. Within it are murals of Bonampak, Mexico. Led to the ruins by Indians in 1945, the photographer, Giles Healey, was the first non–Mayan to view the site. Of particular interest for children is the Fossil Study Center, an interactive learning environment where kids can find prehistoric skeletons or go on a fossil hunt using a computer to plot their strategy. There are also excellent Calusa, Seminole, and Timucuan Indian exhibits and a reconstructed Florida cave.

Location:	Museum Road and Newell Drive on the University of Florida campus
Hours:	Monday through Saturday 10–5, Sunday 1–5, closed Christmas
Fees:	No charge, donations welcome
Phone:	(352) 392–1721

The University Library has an excellent collection of the works, writings, and papers of several of Florida's authors including three members of Florida's Writer's Hall of Fame: Zora Neale Hurston, John D. MacDonald, and Marjorie Kinnan Rawlings. Another major reason to visit the Library is the Creative Writing Manuscript Collection which shows the writing process through drafts, edits, and changes of the works of hundreds of writers, including Truman Capote.

Location:	Smathers Library East on the University of Florida Campus
Hours:	Monday to Friday, 9-4:30. Closed state holidays
Fees:	No charge
Phone:	(352) 392–0321

The *Samuel P. Harn Museum of Art* collection includes 20th-century contemporary American paintings and prints, African, Indian, pre-Columbian, and Asian collections. Be sure to ask about the terra cotta sculpture from central Nigeria that dates from between 815–95 B.C. And that's just one example from the remarkable collection!

Location:	Southwest 34th Street and Hull Road on the University of Florida campus
Hours:	Tuesday through Friday 11–5, Saturday 10–5, Sunday 1–5, closed major holidays
Fees:	No charge, donations welcome
Phone:	(352) 392–9826

Starting in the early 1880s, the *Devil's Millhopper State Geological Site* has been a tourist attraction. It is a 120 foot deep sinkhole, probably the largest in the State since it covers a five acre area. It is estimated that it was formed over 10,000 years ago. First, take the half mile walk around the sinkhole. Then, climb into it. Some of the items that have been found here include fossil shark teeth and fossilized remains of extinct land animals—some of which are now displayed in the nearby Florida Museum of Natural History. Now that you've seen a giant sinkhole, learn about them at the nearby Visitor Center.

Location:	4732 Millhopper Road
Hours:	Daily 9–5
Fees:	$2 per vehicle
Phone:	(352) 955–2008

Make time to walk into a 62 acre woodland complete with meadows, butterflies, and hummingbirds. The *Kanapaha Botanical Gardens* were established in 1978 and contain one of the fourteen major gardens. We particularly enjoy the wildflower walk. The gardens include the largest bamboo collection in Florida and the largest herb garden in the Southeast. An adaptive reuse has been made of a large sinkhole. It is now a sunken garden! For a delightful walk, visit the water gardens with their water falls, streams, and bridges.

Location:	4625 Southwest 63rd Boulevard
Hours:	Monday, Tuesday, and Friday 9–5, Wednesday, Saturday, and Sunday 9–sunset
Fees:	Adults $3, children 6–13 $2
Phone:	(352) or (352) 372–4981

Micanopy

Once the site of an Indian village, Micanopy is one of Florida's oldest towns. The community is now attracting artists and artisans to its historic district. In 1991, a romantic comedy entitled *Doc Hollywood,* starring Michael J. Fox, was released. Look carefully at the downtown parade scenes in the movie. Parts of the film were shot on location in Micanopy.

After you have spent time at the *Paynes Prairie State Preserve,* the state may never look quite the same. Florida's State Park System and the Department of Natural Resources have done a near perfect job maintaining the prairie in its historic condition. When you hike along the trails, realize the Preserve is one of only a few locations maintained as the area would have seemed to the earliest settlers, explorers, and Indians. Imagine a herd of buffalo, much larger than the herd you may see, running free across the prairie, perhaps being hunted by an Indian tribe. Or, imagine living here in the 1600s when the Spanish operated a large cattle ranch in the area. Today, the Visitor Center has exhibits and an audiovisual program to increase your appreciation and enjoyment of the area. Bring your binoculars to watch the birds and bring your hiking gear to truly experience the prairie as it once was throughout this section of the state.

Location:	US 441, ten miles south of Gainesville
Hours:	Daily 8–sunset
Fees:	$3.25 per vehicle with up to eight people
Phone:	(352) 466–3397

Hawthorne/Cross Creek

Marjorie Kinnan Rawlings came to Florida's Cracker Country and stayed to lovingly record many of its strengths and frailties. Mrs. Rawlings' career in Florida began when she sold a Florida Cracker story to *Scribner's Magazine* in the late 1920s. Maxwell Perkins liked her work and encouraged her to continue writing about the isolation of the pioneer farm families in this part of Florida. From her vantage point on Cross Creek, Mrs. Rawlings told of her love of the land and shared the touching, classic story of *The Yearling*. She won the hearts of readers everywhere, as well as a Pulitzer Prize for that work.

Marjorie Kinnan Rawlings at Cross Creek

At the *Marjorie Kinnan Rawlings State Historic Site,* visitors can tour the author's home where she wrote from 1928 until 1941. A simple Cracker structure, the frame house was built around 1890 with a raised floor and pitched roof. Walk through her gardens and the orange grove. If you have a chance read *Cross Creek* and *The Yearling* before your visit—or look at the videos. You will hear her words and remember her work as you spend time in this beautiful and peaceful setting.

Location:	Off County Road 325
Hours:	**Grove and Gardens:** Daily 9–5. **House Tours:** July through October, Thursday through Sunday 10–4
Fees:	**Grounds:** No charge. **Tours:** Adults $2, children 6–12 $1
Phone:	(352) 466–9273

Ocala

Ocala is at the center of some of the finest horse country in the nation. There are over 500 thoroughbred facilities in the area. The equine industry is a $1 billion business employing more than 29,000 people. Over the past decade, Ocala horse breeding and training farms have produced several Kentucky Derby winners. Drive along scenic Highway 301 for a beautiful first look at the industry. One reason there are so many horse farms in the area is the high quality of the grass. Water is naturally filtered through layers of limestone, providing trace minerals which help develop the animals' strong bones. If you visit in the autumn, it is possible to simply stop along the fence posts and watch these animals being exercised and trained—and watch them watching you.

Appleton Museum of Art houses a collection spanning 5,000 years. There are excellent pieces from Africa, the Orient, South and Central America. In addition, be sure to see the 19th century decorative arts collection and the European paintings and sculpture. The Antiquities Gallery, just beyond the entrance, includes a pre–Dynastic Egyptian storage jar, ca. 3300 BC.

Location:	4333 Northeast Silver Springs Boulevard
Hours:	Tuesday through Saturday 10–4:30, Sunday 1–5. Closed major holidays.
Fees:	Adults $3, students with valid ID $2.
Phone:	(352) 236–7100

Don Garlits was one of the major pioneers of drag racing. He developed and raced the rear engine, top fueled dragster. The ***Don Garlits' Museum of Drag Racing*** features racing exhibits and memorabilia as well as a vintage collection of drag racers. The museum preserves the history of drag racing, one of the original forms of auto racing known to man and restores and preserves historical vehicles. The collection includes race cars and memorabilia from the early days of drag racing to the present. Antique vehicles included are classic Fords, and 1950s and 1960s muscle cars. Children particularly like the exotic design of the drag racing cars.

Location:	13700 Southwest 16th Avenue
Hours:	Daily 9–5, closed Christmas
Fees:	**Drag Racing Museum:** Adults $7.50, seniors over 55 $6, children 3–12 $3. **Antique Autos Only**: Adults $5, children 3–12 $3. **Combination Ticket:** Adults $10, children 3–12 $3
Phone:	(352) 245–8661

Eustis

The *Ocala National Forest* is a gem. It was established in 1908 and is the oldest National Forest east of the Mississippi and is the southernmost national forest in the country. For a detailed map, contact the Visitors Center in advance. A few of our favorite activities include canoeing down Juniper Creek or hiking along the Ocala National Recreation Trail that winds north to south through the middle of the forest. Stop at the ranger station for details about day–hike access points. The Forest includes more than 300,000 acres of untamed springs, winding streams, and natural lakes.

Location:	Highway 19, 13 miles from Eustis
Hours:	Daily 9-5, every day but Christmas
Fees:	No charge. Detailed map: $5.50. Canoe Rentals at Juniper Springs Recreation Area: $21.25 for a 4-5 hour trip down Juniper Creek for 2-3 people. Boats and people transported back to the starting point.
Phone:	(352) 625–7470

As we leave you to enjoy a canoe ride in serene and peaceful Ocala National Forest, we hope you take a few minutes to think about the amazing diversity of our state. From the international bustle of Miami to the calm of the forest, from the pristine beaches to the world-class recreation in central Florida—it's a perfect place to explore!

A canoe outing, ca. 1870s

Index

An Uncommon Guide to Florida

Photographic Credits

Charles Hosmer Morse Museum of
  American Art, Winter Park, Florida
Florida
  — Department of Commerce
  — Division of Tourism
  — Photography Archives
Henry Morrison Flagler Museum
Orange County Historical Museum
Ringling Bros. and Barnum & Bailey
  Circus
U.S. Library of Congress